See for your Self

Zen Mindfulness for the Next Generation

ii

"Be the change that you want to see in the world"

- Mohandas Gandhi

"You'll just have to see it for yourselves. What other way is there?"

- Zen Master Lin-Chi

iv

Dedicated to the earth

Copyright © 2011
ISBN 978-0615651941
San Francisco, CA
Original cover design by Kellen Breen
Edited by Ryan Breen, Kimberly Floyd & Don Dianda II

vi

Contents

Preface: For the Reader

Chapter 1: I Had it All, or So I Thought

Chapter 2: Our World Today

Chapter 3: Consciousness, the Ego, and the Self

      - Human Beings: Not Human Doings

      - Alienation

Chapter 4: What Lies Ahead

Chapter 5: Meditation

Chapter 6: Beyond Knowing

Chapter 7: Space & Faith

Chapter 8: Spontaneity

Chapter 9: Surrender

Chapter 10: Letting Go

Chapter 11: Equanimity

Chapter 12: Presence

Chapter 13: Impermanence

Chapter 14: Karma

Chapter 15: The Sword of Mindfulness

Chapter 16: Nature

Chapter 17: The Spectrum of Darkness & Light

Chapter 18: Blow Down the Walls

Chapter 19: Visualizations & Practices

Epilogue: Koan on the Great Way

viii

For the Reader

> A monk asked: "How does one get emancipated?"
> The master replied: "Who has ever put you in bondage?"
> Monk: "What is the Pure Land?"
> Master: "Who has ever defiled you?"
> Monk: "What is Nirvana?"
> Master: "Who has ever subjected you to birth and death?"
>   - Zen Master Shih-t'ou

This book is a conversation about walking your own spiritual path in life. Through the masters – the Buddha and others – it is possible to discern the ways to genuine peace, wisdom, and balance. Turning inward, raising our level of consciousness, becoming more aware, and focusing on being right here, right now, is how we go about deepening.[1] Being mindful, that is, paying attention to our inner realms moment-by-moment, and giving right effort to our sterling practice, we move forward, inward, and in the end realize that everything we ever longed for resides within – it always has. Seeing and feeling it first, we wish to seek it: What we find is our own nature.

> What we sow and how we tend what we sow determines the lushness of the harvest, the ripeness of the fruit.

How open are you to self-empowerment or to gaining inner wisdom? Do you wish to uncover these qualities? For they are here and they represent just a few of the small, innate treasures one can reap from inwardly seeking. *Through this book, we learn how to go below the surface to touch the deep ocean of our inner realms and to remain in contact with them throughout daily life. We learn to let this peace make itself known and so, with time, we become it.* Seeing reality as it is, speaking impeccably, living in a state of acceptance, maintaining balance, all of these qualities are presented naturally when we learn to be in contact with our inner depths.[2] It may seem outlandish or undoable, but with practice and an open mind, you will be surprised at what naturally springs from your inner Self. Give it the space it needs, stay open, and keep reading.

I encourage you to read slowly and to take breaks between chapters. After ten or twenty pages go outside, let the words seep in and then return. The book can work on you if you let it. It has a power of its own that will show itself to you, through you, sometimes when you least expect it. There is an energetic subtext that can reorganize you. Slow down a little and try to match the wave- length of the writing. It will have much more of an effect that way and it will enrich your experience. Stay open. When we remain open, we allow things to take root. They can work on us without us ever having to do or know anything. This is the simple magic, the innateness, the 'thusness' of awareness.

The process is not necessarily rational, nor is it irrational. The path is non-linear, it reflects the true nature of the infinite space we move through: inconceivable, intricately interconnected, and most certainly beyond the narrow confines of the clinging ego-mind. What comes up, comes up. We feel it and we witness it. The more we allow the words on the page to roam freely, to root, the deeper we go, and the more we uncover. The book reflects this approach:

> Out of nowhere the mind and everything it perceives comes forth.[3]

Every day, things appear that reflect what previously was read, whether we know it at that moment or not. These instances become keys for our deepening. Keys can come in the form of a smile, a realization, a laugh, a sneeze, a word, a soaring red-tailed hawk. Even a half eaten cheeseburger can open what needs to be opened inside of us. Keys are all around, hidden within each passing moment. We are what is important for the process to unfold. When we realize and accept a key, the process deepens and we begin to see the interweaving nature of life. What remains essential though, is *our* continued openness, and eventually, our wish to walk through the door. No key has ever opened a stone wall.[4]

There is deep, ancient wisdom presented within the lines and phrases of this book. The voices of many past masters and seekers appear in the form of quotes and radiating words that shook my view of life as I navigated my internal regions. There is no prophecy, no merciful or patronizing God, no fortunetelling, just the conveyance of a door for us to find our own way – the Way, in life.[5] When the book is over, we will have walked to the doorstep and our journey, our direct experience, will have just begun. This life – the one I am experiencing – certainly has:

> It is important for the reader to note that there is no discrepancy between 'you' and 'I'. I am on my path and this book reflects what I have felt, seen, passed below and dived

through. There is no teacher here, no borders, no authority figure – just an intimate exchange of words. And yet, when we remove the boundaries, the book becomes an evocative calling of sorts to the one within you who is ready to move into a new arena of experience – who is ready to step into this conversation.[6]

What motivates us to seek a deeper Self? Disenchantment with the shallow nature of society, an adventurous heart, swaying out of balance, a sense of lacking, too much materialism, depression, a disconnection from the world, and a need to connect to something real all push us toward seeking some sort of remedy. We may be divinely inspired, we may have had a near-death experience, or we may just be bored with living a life conditioned and confined by mainstream culture. Whatever the case, it doesn't matter. All that counts is that you and I are open and ready to find inner balance through turning our energy back in on itself and learning how to be the witness below all thoughts.

The power of the process to make the shift is in your hands. Your ability to remain open to what comes and your wish to see beyond the confines of conditioned existence will greatly enhance the experience of this book. The pace is patience, the rationale can be… beyond conventional. The writing is expansive, for that is its purpose – to tear down the mental walls you and I have made.

Anyone can wake up to the life of turning in at any time, at any age and under any circumstance. It has nothing to do with anyone or anything else. Deepening oneself is a wonderful, practical experience that truly enriches life in every way imaginable. But it takes dedication. The practitioner has to want to see more, to be present more, while remaining willing to surrender and to be less. We are going to have to be more honest, wiser, happier, more receptive, and more open – something that was and still is difficult for me! We are going to have to want to see through the dream and see reality as it is. And most importantly, we must practice. It may not be what you expect, but you will learn to love the unexpected, the non-linear, and the unconventional. [7]

There is much wisdom to be uncovered in the world and it is all waiting for us novices.[8] The more we dive in, the more appears, and the more we melt. Many of us have been sleeping, unaware of what there is beyond our small view of what we deem important and what we are conditioned to pay attention to in life. There is nothing wrong with this, except for the fact that we remain unaware, and so we live and die. This isn't doom and gloom: relax, this is how it is. The quicker we realize the dream we are in, the quicker we can begin to make real, positive change, the more we can be present.

The following chapters are comprised of practices, personal struggles, words, and advice for life on the path. Starting with a personal context and examining the parts of who we are and then going into meditation, we lay the groundwork for our stroll into being present, and also our journey into our internal wilderness. Delving into the chapter on beyond knowing, accepting the scope of mindfulness and the non-intellectual nature of the process, we examine certain pieces, the gems of the road. These will help keep us on the path and moving forward; and examining letting go, space, surrender, balance, impermanence, will help push us toward a greater understanding of being and what it means to live a true, fruitful life. Looking at each of these aspects deeply, we begin to learn more about ourselves and the universe we move through (and that also moves through us).

Follow along and remain open to what you read in the coming pages. Let down any inner guards or doubts, just for a few moments, and see what happens. Take a few conscious breaths every now and then. Not just for the book, but for life itself. Each step we take from where we are now toward complete consciousness is a step in the *Right* direction.[9] Each step brings its own rewards. Sometimes these rewards are tangible, and sometimes they are simply a shift in our openness – our ability to see clearly and to experience life more intimately. When we shift, we are not receiving any fish or bones. We are learning how to fish – how to create our nourishment, our happiness, our balance ourselves.

The year is 2012, and yet, the calling, the process, and the goal remain the same as always. Turning inward, getting in touch with who and what we really are underneath the surface, is what must be undertaken. Through such an endeavor, we learn to be in this world, but not completely of it. We learn to live life in the here and now. We learn to let go, to allow, and thus, to enrich every moment. If we can close our eyes and feel this truth just a little, then we are ready to move on.

Stay open and let the words seep in. You don't have to do anything else.

You never know,

Space is canvas,

Being is everything.

These words should have new meaning for you soon.

I Had it All, or So I Thought

"Do the difficult things while they are easy and do the great things while they are small."

- Lao Tzu

"Everyday is a journey, and the journey itself is home."

- Matsuo Basho

Growing up in a well-to-do American family is materially comfortable. Family troubles aside, and they can be considerable, life is full of pleasure: desires are satisfied, drinks guzzled, and fanciful whims gained. There are high school football games, schooldays, workdays, sex, travelling, television, Fourth of July celebrations, drama, weekend all-nighters, jokes, cliques, victories, and defeats. Like a giant cliché, life unfolds, and it unfolds around a focal point: me – I – a separate ego. From here good and bad, love and hate, sad, mad, happy, despair, upbeat, low, subject, object, outside, come together to form one's life experience. To keep some form of sanity, we follow our mind and attempt to gratify its wants and needs as a way to find fulfillment and success. We create stories and follow them. We listen to our thoughts intently to the point where we eventually become them. We go for more and more.[10] But is that it? Is there any marrow to it, or is it all about trying to have an even better time or seeking a higher position on a ladder? I found out. Coming home at three in the morning tired, intoxicated, full of shallow thoughts and loaded with cheap laughs, my life was passing before my eyes.

During my first two years in college, I often had the urge to 'black out,' literally. Though I wasn't conscious enough to be aware of it at the time, I wanted to be able to float through life, running from painful experiences that had rooted themselves into my psyche. The path at the time was simply to ignore any stirrings within and to keep going, to press on, to focus on money and being accepted within the constructs of the society in which I found myself. To do everything but communicate how I really felt, or for that matter, even to know how I felt.[11] These were the values. Sure, I had to do well in school and/or make money, but those were externalities that had nothing to do with what was driving me (and on a macroscopic level, parts of our culture), in contrast to facing up and turning in to examine myself. I was so compulsive, impulsive – always trying to escape or be numb or tough.[12] If I needed to keep myself busy then I could dive into work, watch television, play videogames, plan a trip to Vegas, fiddle with my smart-phone, none of which addressed my seething unease. No, instead of learning to be present, I dove into the culture I found myself in, I donned the mask,[13] and I kept wading out more deeply into the fog that surrounded me, totally blind to what lay buried beneath the facade and believing that my blindness was the standard way to go about *this* life.

It seemed that the more I was able to close-off, the more alcohol or drugs I was able to consume, and the more money I was able to surround myself with, the more attention I garnered – the more I moved up some invisible ladder. I was armoring myself and feeling more comfortable with the things I appeared to be gaining. I felt 'cooler.' I felt stronger, and so I continued to build upon this illusory pile. But in reality I was being weak and I was running away from myself as fast as I could possibly go. What's funny to me as I look back on that time was how upside down everything was. How could being blacked out connote any form of strength? How could suppressing painful memories be powerful? How could living in my thoughts and hiding behind the things I did or the judgments I created, be rewarding? It didn't make a lot of sense to me. Looking back, it seemed that the culture I was buying into was telling me, "the faster you are able to run away from being present, the more quickly you can scamper away from who you are below the surface, the better off you will be, and the more things you can hide behind."

> But this party line is simply a figment of imagination – a creation that is as substantial and sturdy as a sandcastle. Something was shifting inside me. I wasn't aware of what it was or how it was working. But I began to question what was going on around me and why I went along without checking in with myself – without questioning the narrative spinning in my head.

I changed my life and woke up during my junior year of college. I had had enough. The drinking didn't do it for me. The partying didn't do it for me. Vegas, Miami, and L.A. didn't do it for me. The sensual possibilities didn't do it for me. I felt completely strange and insubstantial in my own body. Everything I had created, my ego, my friendships, my internal wiring, my identity – aspects of my external being I had spent years cultivating, shaping and re-shaping – were just the bones of a paper tiger in the face of the stirrings of what lay buried beneath. I was blind. I had been living in a dream and I was finally beginning to realize it.

I come from a wealthy family, and life was beyond comfortable growing up. I felt physically fit, attractive, sociable, intelligent, perfectly capable of leading some sort of idealistic life following a well-groomed path. On the surface, everything *looked* great. How could I complain then? What could possibly be wrong? A college degree, loads of friends, money, travel, flexibility, and any form of ingestible escape were all at my grasping fingertips.

Looking back, I see the attractiveness of such a lifestyle: an existence in which one is constantly re-filling his or her cup, satisfying each and every craving.[14] It seems very appealing. But, for some *strange* reason, it felt incomplete, even shallow, and the more I attempted to reach outside myself for things, the more apparent the incompleteness became.

The slow change within my heart had been an ongoing process. There had been an upwelling of feeling and emotion when I had been alone hiking in the hills or swimming in the ocean. Also, brief moments of disconnect from my social life allowed questions concerning what I was doing to bubble up. But fear and doubt coincided with these thoughts. So, naturally I did what I was good at: I dove back into my life with added vigor. I denied. I suppressed all my inner yearnings with more alcohol, more drugs, and more meaningless relationships. I searched for more of the same to fill the growing inner void and outer disconnection, feeding my ego, only to have it come back to me over and over again. There was something deep inside that persisted in repelling my unconscious overtures. Though I did not realize it at the time, my Self[15] was saving me from myself. How could I realize what was going on? It seemed so strange. I had everything, but then, why this feeling of meaninglessness? Why complain? I was a lucky man, right? What else was there to get, to have, to experience? I had it all, right? The answer, though it took time, was very simple. There is nowhere to go, nothing to do, nothing to see, and no one to follow: there is nothing other than learning to be in *this life, in this moment.*

Some inner intelligence could foresee my future. It knew that I was on the wrong path. No matter how rich, powerful, or likeable I ever became, 'something' knew that these ghosts would never bring true happiness, lasting connection, or unadulterated freedom. My existence would continue to resemble that of a hungry, impulsive ghost: running to this and that only to have it float through my body and out again. I would live this way, deluded into thinking it was the only way of being, my entire life. My existence would be a shadow that would never come to know its real host or feel the intimate relationship one could have with this very life.[16] No – this was not for me. The truth lay beyond all these things. Little pleasures were not a permanent solution, they were part of the never ending, cyclical problem.

If time passes in the blink of an eye, how could insubstantial *things* be more valuable than the *present moment?*

One early morning after going out and drinking, I came home feeling slightly ill. I crawled into bed and passed out, something many of us can relate to. In the night I dreamed that a powerful, jet-black snake had been sucking vital energy from the back of my neck. Its muscles pulsated with each drink. All I could do was grab and pull, but to no avail. My energy had been sapped. I was horrified because I knew that to let the snake win – to be overcome – meant losing my soul and spirit to something that was not me – a 'vampiric' fabrication of me that would feed on more and more fabrications – a true soul and spirit sucker. With all my might I finally pulled its fangs from my back and threw it to the ground. It writhed and wiggled in front of me, making a hissing sound. I was truly disgusted. Suddenly it began moving toward me to attack again and attach itself to me once more. It was tenacious, pugnacious, and it was bent on returning. I am no master, but the life-sucking black snake had to go.

This profound, adrenaline-pumping dream shook me to my core. I was disengaged from whatever chains were holding me back and the ensuing space allowed me to act spontaneously the next day without regret.[17] In the morning I packed my things and left. My inner Self had shown me some truth. There was no denying it and I felt compelled to move toward open space. To continue down my path without change would have meant to live my life in complete delusion and denial.[18] I changed my life that day, walking away from many of my closest acquaintances. It is was not an easy process, but the clarity that came with change, especially drastic, tough change, was more than enough of a confirmation for me.

Jumping headlong into wide-open space.

The initial process of dropping everything and leaving was very difficult. As I said, there was nothing amazing about completely changing my life and being ok with not knowing where I was, who I was, or what I was doing. It took some time for me to adjust to this and to appreciate the value and clarity of not knowing. When the dust settled, I felt empowered and, 'shockingly' life still came and went as it always had, moment-to-moment.[19] For the first time I could see through some of my attachments. I could see through the glamour with which I was once enamored and I was able to catch brief glimpses of feelings I had not quite experienced fully before. Light and darkness, the moments I deemed comfortable or uncomfortable, appeared more brilliantly than before and I felt that I had begun to step out of my perpetuated state of grey for the first time. All the cycles, all the neurotic behaviors, all the disservices to the body were cast out and laid bare before the growing light of internally focused, inquisitive observation. This was the beginning of my path of awareness.[20]

Each of us is different. Some will not have to do anything like this, and some will have to do more. There is no right or wrong and this is an interesting conclusion when it begins to settle. All that is required is honesty and true listening to the stirrings within. There is no other barometer than that, no other energy with which to power our movements. If the heart-mind is given room and given open inner ears, it will show us the way to the Self, the path we must take. It is that simple.[21]

And on the other side, this process in its entirety, applies to everyone. All external pleasures we attach ourselves to our delusions – images, projections, comfortable thought forms – that keep us plugged into our small mind. The mind is always running. And without witnessing the rampant movement and disassociating ourselves from it, we will never be satisfied – we will run and run, and then run some more. We will strive and strive to fill our cups. We will always look ahead for the next thing; the next car, the next mate, the next job, the next happy hour, the next externality we can grab and hold onto. This unending cycle will repeat our entire

24

lives and we will not notice that our eyes are closed, enraptured by the dream. Life will ultimately follow suit. It will pass us by and we will continue trying to comfort ourselves among all the questions, all the unfinished things. Our ghost will hunger for more and we, believing we are the ghost and not knowing anything else, will keep going, on and on and on.

Seeing the snake before succumbing to it was crucial. By just seeing it, I could begin to make a change. Telling the snake, a metaphor for one's small, created ego, "I see you," and being able to recognize it throughout the day is just as effective. For the ego, like most other things in the world of form, is a mere creation. It is who we *think* we are and it is propped up only by our continual feeding. And by 'feeding' I mean our identification with it. But this creation, this shadow is not who we are. Every time we act impulsively, every time we judge, every time we resist what naturally comes and thus identify with it, we are feeding ego and making it stronger. We are losing touch with our inner core and stepping out into a fog.

It is possible to stop feeding our egotistical view of the world through watching our actions, feelings, and thoughts, becoming a witness of the ego rather than the unconscious actor. Practicing impeccable speech, staying present, and going with the flow, are all ways of stopping the trend of ego and initiating change. Witness the mind for a while and see what happens. I often ask myself: Am I truly present? Are my thoughts positive or negative, compassionate or selfish? Do I see the world from my point of view and through my desires, or am I coming from unfettered clarity? Am I open or am I closed?

I learned much about who I was, or more truthfully, who I thought I was. It was interesting to study and watch my ego in action, and I was often taken aback by the nasty thoughts, righteous justifications, and unnecessary dialogue that popped up when I was feeling uncomfortable and abandoning my Self. You may experience something similar, so listen to your heart-mind. Give it space. Allow it to make itself known to you through self-examination and the cultivation of inner stillness. Begin to bring this into all phases of your life, the good and the bad: equanimity knows nothing of the two.

In order to raise awareness, we must be willing to recognize the options before us and the path that lies ahead. This is entirely up to us because in the end, WE are the ones who create everything. WE are the ones who suffer, who feel up, down, and sometimes all over the place. WE are the ones who continue to perpetuate an unfulfilling and fabricated reality. And this is great news of course! Knowing that we are responsible, that we are the cause, and that the unexamined ego is the culprit is the first step. Understanding that we can CHANGE it all through awareness is everything we need to know. There is nothing standing in our way. If we dig deep, if we turn our consciousness back in on itself, we will find an unobstructed openness renewed within the vastness of each moment. Trust this and you will be freed from any internal prison.

Turn in and begin digging. Open up to the possibilities and put down your thoughts.

By no means does turning in mean turning away. We are not neglecting anything. We are not running away from anything. *No, for the first time we will stop running away and relying on a created reality. Turning in means turning toward.* It is powerful. It is a way of claiming our true Self, and it can be done in the midst of all the challenges we perceive and with which we live. Through turning in, such challenges will become practice and eventually we will learn to turn such things into gold through mindfulness – a natural alchemy that is simply a return to our true Self in this moment. It is all so strange, mysterious, and yet utterly necessary.

> "The most beautiful thing we can experience is the mysterious. It is the source of all true art and all science. He to whom this emotion is a stranger, who can no longer pause to wonder and stand rapt in awe, is as good as dead: his eyes are closed."
>
> - Albert Einstein

Empower yourself and unpeel the layers of shallow ego-identification. Release yourself from the small mind and live for the first time. For we are not who we think we are, and things are not what they seem to be.

Two roads, many roads, an infinite number of roads diverged in a forest. Which did you take? Your own. When we walk the path, we can tap into and feel our presence. Life bends towards us intimately without us having to make any effort to make it do so, without having to fight, or control or even know why things are occurring as they are. And we are aware of all that is there before us. If we sincerely continue, we will learn to touch the lives of others meaningfully. What other gift is there than this?

There is absolutely no difference between you and the Buddha, the Buddha and me. We are human beings. We are Buddhas waiting to be unmasked, waiting to step out into the light in *this* life. We are a sage covered in a fine veil, a translucent mask. If we can accept this truth a little, and if we begin practicing mindfulness, we have the opportunity to become awakened beings. What a powerful realization: our cultivated presence is a positive force in this world. All we need to do is step back and see reality as it is without judgment. All that is required is our willingness to turn in, put down our mind, and cultivate an unwavering commitment to the path.

Our heart, our "heart-mind" as Buddha called it, left alone will never fail us. Listen to it, because it sees the endless cycles of doubt and wasted time ahead of us if we continue to follow our rampant *mind* – a tool of great power and great pain depending on how we use it or are used by it. Don't continue the cycle of conditioned existence. Step out and get in touch with yourself. Become aware of suffering in you and in others, and begin by breaking the trend of destructive alcoholism in your family, stopping the gossip in your circle, and protecting the environment through fundamentally and completely accepting the now you inhabit. Look deeply into the *nature* of life as it is, not your subjective version of it, and you will see. Silently watch the mind in this moment and wisdom will unfurl naturally on its own.[22]

When I was sitting on top of a mountain straddling the California-Nevada border and pondering the depth of a

nearby snowfield, I realized something simple: I was free. I
have never laughed so hard, for so long in my life.

I thought I had it all when really I was fumbling down a road
shrouded in haze. It took a profound dream and a sudden move to
shift out of my old life and find a path. There weren't any
fireworks or flowers. There wasn't even a map, just a simple
realization that life would come, whether I wanted it to or not, and
that learning to accept this truth openly was part of the journey. It
became apparent that sitting still and letting go bring about an
opportunity for a moment of clarity, planting the seed for an
internal transformation. I didn't have to do anything but stop and
witness my mind.

Our World Today

"Your vision will become clear only when you can look into your own heart. Who looks outside, dreams; who looks inside, awakes."

- Carl Jung

Oftentimes, in the modern world, we get so caught up in the mechanization of life – brooding on the past, looking to the clock, projecting into the future, stuck on our beliefs and opinions – that we become machines ourselves. Anxiety, attention issues, emotional control, and stress plague us. We fear emptiness and space so much that we find it necessary to fill them with any distraction. Though we may be successful in finding the perfect job or finding the cool group, we lose touch with ourselves.

When I began to examine my mind through meditation and present-moment awareness, I was amazed at the amount of mental noise blasting through my head. There were answers, judgments, thoughts, plans, notions, and opinions, swirling about. I could not sit in silence without thinking of the next activity that needed to be taken care of. On the flip side, when I had quiet time, it was not quiet. There was always a narrative or film playing out through my thoughts. If I had free time, it was never free. Television, thoughts, text messages, assumptions, and fantasies all clouded my sense of reality. Sometimes my mind would act impulsively, leading me toward food, drink, exercise, and other external pleasures that had nothing to do with the present or what I was feeling internally. These externalities did nothing but perpetuate my cycle of suffering.[23] All these things maintained my separation and, like most people, I was completely hooked. Judgment and reaction ruled supreme.

When I practiced mindfulness while driving, I was taken aback by how upset I was when a light turned red or when someone took a right turn into my lane, slowing me down. Why was I so upset? Why did I just lose my cool over that? I was in a hurry, my mind was wandering, and I was not in touch with the deep, still lake of my being lying below the surface. I was too caught up in my created world and too deluded to realize it. On walks too, or while cleaning dishes in my small metallic sink – in the seemingly mundane moments or tasks that fill the majority of all human life – I could not help but notice how easily I could be swept up and away by my internal dialogue.

We all do this to a certain extent. Every day we create and move through a dream rooted in our thoughts. Yes, we have obligations, we have responsibilities, duties to fulfill. Of course, this is the 21st century. But to lose ourselves, to be governed by the rampant mind and our impulses rather than being the still master, is to be run by the dream. To judge, to fight, to resist, to be wrapped in our small selves, is to lose our true power.

> We simply cage our Selves: If we can see the cage, even if it is just a glimpse, we can start to overcome it: The birth of awareness.

In the beginning, witnessing is all that is necessary. Consciously asking ourselves, where is this impulse coming from? Why am I doing this? Am I one hundred percent right here, right now, or am I somewhere else? Asking in a way that is non-judgmental and honest is the key. At first we just watch and learn. As truth comes and we wish to move forward, we begin to deepen. Don't allow the mind to judge harshly. That is a sneaky way for it to reassert itself. Just watch – observe – and get in touch peacefully. Many little 'victories' each day fan our growing awareness – pure consciousness. Be aware, patient, watch, and it will continue to grow.

> Image: the full moon converting the sun's energy into soft light.

We all have our filters of reality. We are conditioned, and we react and judge in a way that reflects our conditioning. An object, an event comes into our zone of awareness, we judge it and we react to it depending on our view of life, our mood, and what ego-form we identify with. We see a tree, boom, it is tall, green, ugly or pretty, wide, strong, crooked, old, full of bugs, too outlandish for the garden, too luscious, a redwood, a palm tree, and much more. What if we just saw "tree?" What if we just see the tree as it is while remaining calm and collected – totally present. This is a simple example but it encapsulates the dynamic of duality and the ego: one in which everything is there but YOU.

> In Zen, non-virtuous action does not simply mean immoral action, rather, it includes all actions undertaken without total presence and thus a clear and unclouded mind.

No matter what we have ever done in life, our true and timeless Self is always here within the mind and the moment. This is radical and ancient wisdom. Letting go of all our formed opinions, the layers of our ego, and our attachments, we reach for the core and the truth becomes evident. In experiencing the Self, what we are underneath the mental stream, our inherent, innate qualities of being, we begin to see the metaphorical heaven on earth moment-to-moment. But know, I can write *about* Self – that is all. The Self can only be experienced, not described. Though I attempt to describe it, I fail. We all must experience it for our Selves.

Consciousness, the Ego, and the Self

"The brain immediately confronts us with its great complexity. The human brain weighs only three to four pounds but contains about 100 billion neurons (& trillions of synapses). Although that extraordinary number is of the same order of magnitude as the number of stars in the Milky Way, it cannot account for the complexity of the brain"[24]

- Gerald D. Fischbach

"With no surroundings there can be no path, and with no path one cannot become free."

- Gary Snyder

The three inner components of the spiritual path are comprised of our level of consciousness (or awareness), the surface level ego, and the underlying, natural, true, and balanced Self.[25] Though I speak of three distinct pieces, they are all one. Our ego, which is a mental creation formed through conditioned existence and unconscious action, blocks us from realizing our inner core. The mind is the tool we rely on in life, and through the perpetuation of this dependent relationship without the practice of awareness, the mind becomes our master. It usurps us in our unconsciousness, and then it keeps us there. We are under the spell of the ego. This is why consciousness is the doorway beyond the veil of the ego – beyond our unconsciousness.

Consciousness brings forth the innate Self. When we can see through the ego, the noise, the emotions, the reactions, the opinions, and the judgments, we are essentially free and so we are able to reach down and contact our true nature. Through turning the light of consciousness inwards and daily mindfulness practice, our consciousness expands and we become increasingly who we are underneath the surface.

> Embodying the Self requires effort. The mind will always try to reassert itself. Mindfulness and clear vision will make this truth evident. All one has to do after he has seen the duality, the ego, and the Self, is to take note and observe – to be the space that is open to all things and allows the myriad to melt into one.

A profound question for us to ask ourselves is, "What am I?" This is not a question of identity, of 'who' – no – the question

"What am I?" goes far beyond such notions. The question's purpose is to aid us in our quest to look beyond, or, rather to turn the light inward. It cuts through the surface to point out all the things we identify with; race, gender, height, ideology, political inclination, nationality, religion, and so forth – a series of externalities to which we attach ourselves and thus *literally create ourselves*. When we truly – sit – stop – let go – and reflect on the question of, "What am I," we begin to see reality as it is. There is something else, something far more substantial, [26] going on within the vastness of the Self and the vastness of the present moment.

"What am I?" utterly destroys notions, ideas, and identities we have created. We are none of these surface-level entities born out of shallow perceptions and judgments. With this clear insight, we see the illusory nature of identity, of 'who we think we are.' We are not a series of mental creations and conditionings. This is false and yet it is how a large majority of the world lives. There is something much deeper than what meets the senses – and that of course is, the '*What.*'

The ego and 'the who' that we think we are, are synonymous – they are creations of the mind. They are also *of* this world. Living amongst the mental projections is okay, but it is not the ultimate reality we inhabit.[27] How so? Go out at night and look at the stars, walk into a forest, or sit in meditation for twenty minutes: You will find your answers *there*. Blame and forgiveness, money, problems, and praise, when placed against *this background,* melt away into wide-open space.[28] The continuation of human evolution will not come from our illusory lifestyles and old habitual ways of living. It will come from a volitional, conscious decision to reach into the depths of what we are and to let the entity flourish.

We must look beyond the veil of the ego. We must be willing to let go and look a little deeper to see through and into 'the what' within us all. What you are is up to you to discover.[29] The process of seeking is the process of getting in touch with this 'What.' Throughout your day, look back onto this question. Begin to witness the ego as it is. Remove yourself, little by little from the 'who,'[30] and begin to realize the 'What.'[31] It is within this 'What' that we begin to uncover the true Self.

"When the mind keeps tumbling
How can vision be anything but blurred?
Stop the mind even for a moment
And all becomes transparently clear!
The moving mind is polishing mud bricks.
In stillness find the mirror!"

- Han Shan Te-Ching

Consciousness

Consciousness in the spiritual dimension is the experience of being fully present and totally aware of one's inner and outer experience moment-to-moment. It *is* the action and the direct experience of listening, watching, observing, and witnessing which leads us down deeper toward the Self. Anything that we are aware of at a given moment, either inside or out, makes up our conscious experience. We lose touch with consciousness when the mind is in charge – thinking, worrying, judging, resisting, acting impulsively, suppressing, dreaming, inhabiting the future, inhabiting the past – remaining in a place that is subjective and closed rather than open and clear.

> Presence, mindfulness, awareness, concentration, acceptance of what is are your power words and phrases for raising your level of consciousness on a daily basis. If you can live your life in a way that reflects these principles as I am referring to them, then life will flow as it is. Breathing and being is the way.

What is going on inside you throughout the day? Do you take time to look inside and see what is *actually* occurring? Raising consciousness means becoming a watcher of what is happening inside you 24/7. It is the process of taking inventory. Watching with no judgment and no resistance, just pure mindfulness. When you feel angry, you label it the emotion, anger. You watch it, and you sit with it for a moment.

When you judge, you label it anger and then fall into the trap of incessant thought about what is happening, or worse, you criticize yourself for being angry and drive yourself further away from the path. The important thing to remember is to embody the watcher – to see what is happening and just to observe. This may take a great deal of practice, but the fruits are well worth the effort and the patience.

Consciously seeing through our delusions is like being let out of a mentally based prison. It expands who we are and blows down the walls we constantly erect around ourselves. Every time we overcome a delusion, it is like pushing the fence of our backyard back ten yards, walking up to the barrier, and looking through the cracks at the surrounding infinite wilderness. With sustained practice and thus increased consciousness, we see what is driving us and we gain a deeper perspective of life that had been beyond our capacity of living weeks and months before.[32] Past fears and old abuses – seen clearly – melt into insubstantiality. We are going beyond all things and entering into an entirely new dimension of existence that has always been right in front of us. No matter how I or anyone else describes consciousness or conscious living, it can never do justice. Consciousness must be directly experienced by you and you alone! And it can be at any moment of one's life – like now… or… now! You must be the one who sees for him or her Self.

Small Mind: The Ego

The mind, or in a physical sense, the brain, controls each and every one of our bodily functions while maintaining all incoming and outgoing mental movements, thoughts, and perceptions. The mind has been our greatest tool in conquering the world, the animal kingdom, and of course, conquering each other. It has given us the greatest technological advancements, and the most moving prose, but it also does much more than that. Our heavy reliance on the mind allows it to run our lives and thus our being, completely. There is no need to do or to judge in the thousands of different ways that we do. There is no need to see the world as one that is evil and that is out to get us. That is a projection of the mind that moves us to act in a way that is defensive and selfish.

We rely on the mind more than anything. Where elephants use their size and cheetahs use their speed, the human uses his mind. It is our command and control center. From our heartbeat to our sexual desires, the mind does it all, no questions asked. However, through complete reliance on our mind, we lose our inherent connection to all things. It distorts reality and turns life into a constant narrative, and soon we are hypnotized by the streaming film passing above our brow. When we become enamored with our thoughts, rather, when we create a reality within thought, we become stuck, we lose our Selves. The world disappears, the now disappears, and we fall into a prison.

The mind's offspring, the ego, or who we perceive ourselves to be, reigns supreme. We become so identified with our ego that it clouds our ability to see things just as they are. Our ego judges, reacts, and separates us from all that is. We create likes and dislikes, and we act in a manner that reflects a polarized vision. We must gratify our senseless desires or we must act on a defensive aversion. Before we know it, everything becomes centered around us – everything has an explanation, everything must be conquered for the sake of the ego.

"A man is a method, a progressive arrangement; a selecting

principle, gathering his like to him; wherever he goes."
- Ralph Waldo Emerson

If we do not see this, our ego will continue to run our lives. It is a classic example of the master being taken over by his machine, and if we are able to stop for a moment, this dynamic becomes very apparent. This is not bad or evil, this is just what we do – what we have always done. The question is, can *we* go beyond the ego? Can we practice witnessing its movements (raising our consciousness), and thus reach down toward the Self? Through the ego we become so absorbed with the small stuff, we become so attached to ourselves, that any depth fades below the surface and we are left to struggle in the crashing waves of illusory thought.

You can end the power of the small mind – the ego – the monkey mind. You can break the clinging ego through mindfulness and present awareness. In a way, we are seeking because we wish to free ourselves from the mind and regain our natural consciousness – to regain our connection to the world and the universe from which we were born and thus to live in the unobstructed present. The ego, then, is a wonderful tool for us because we can watch its movements and increase our awareness of the vast body lying below.

The Self[33]

The Self represents the deepest[34] nature within each and every one of us. The Self lays dormant, yet it is always present, waiting to be uncovered through mindful attention. The Self is a pure way of being. One who lives through the Self is totally conscious, present, and in touch. He or she is in this world but not of it. She is at peace, open, and receptive – mindful and aware. When she enters, her presence is felt. The Self is a way of being. Peeling the layers of ego away is how we get to our inner core. This core, the Self, is the deep ocean of calm, balance, and joy inherently within us. To touch the core is to know what the ancients referred to as divine, to know the true power of being. But we have lived in a world that knows very little about such things. Our conditioned existence, our society, and most importantly, our egos, are obstructions lying before those who walk the path of mindfulness. Embodying the Self and becoming more conscious go hand-in-hand with practice and sincere effort.

In a way, the Self implies reverence and respect. It does not appear through the small mind, because the small mind is child's play compared to the infinite nature of the Self. Zen teachings refer to the dynamic between the small mind and the Self as one between small mind and Big mind. Small mind represents a small, Velcro-like entity that sticks, gets bogged down, and remains in a self-perpetuated state of restlessness. It attaches, it resists, it fights, it plans, and it does everything and anything to keep the conveyer belt going. The Self shines. It is the complete opposite, a diamond that goes beyond anything the ego or the intellect can comprehend. Patient, intuitive, humble, wise, and all-encompassing, the Self flows with life and accepts what occurs as it is. Its view is one of focused vastness and it sees our place within the grand scheme of the interconnected universe. It is balanced and even-keeled, accepting praise and criticism as well as ups and downs as they are. Conscious, vibrant, and present, the Self sits wrapped within each human being.

"Enlightenment must come little by little-otherwise it would overwhelm."

- Idries Shah

Like an iceberg you exist in the world. You are completely unaware of the scope of what you truly are underneath the surface. And the beautiful thing is, the ego and the Self and the consciousness that is necessary for witnessing, are part of the same interrelated existence. These are just terms and over time they will all inevitably dissipate into direct experience.

Image: Roots in the ground, a mind of sky.

Taking root in the present and being is all we have to do to begin. Letting go of who we think we are and opening up to the vastness of space is all that is required of us. The more and more we do this throughout our daily life, the more we deepen, the less ego we identify with. Grounding, opening, grounding, opening, and then breathing going back to our day a little less of who we were and a little more of what we are.[35]

Human Beings, not Human Doings

I think, therefore... I am often not.

I do, therefore... I am often gone.

We can always find a way to get through life, to take care of what needs to be taken care of, to suppress what bothers us, to be something else, or to go somewhere else outside of who we are and what we are experiencing in any moment. There are always avenues for us to walk down to distract us or to cover up a sense of loss within. It is easy to find all sorts of distractions, and that is why we constantly gravitate toward this way of going through the motions. We walk into the fog and then we choose to stay in it, though we are often not *aware of it*. This way of living becomes ingrained in us and we follow it mechanically, automatically, systematically.

We do something, but were we really there? Are we human beings or are we human doings? Are we present, aware and open? Do we flow with the moment? Or are we closed off, fantasizing, planning, manipulative, removed, lost, and judgmental? These questions require nothing but honesty, clarity, and deep looking into our actions, our words, and fundamentally, our thoughts.

Be aware and be honest. This is a very simple initial step of recognition. Are you a human being or a human doing throughout your day? There is no wrong answer here, just inner reflection. Within this reflection, you move toward being. You have the choice to see or not to see, to be aware or not to be aware. Every human being has the ability to turn all situations into gold, not through denial or false happiness, but through learning to be and feel completely – to suck the marrow out of everything and learn to be fully present and aware in all situations.

> "Thus the master is available to all people and doesn't reject anyone. He is ready to use all situations and doesn't waste anything. This is called embodying the light."
> - Tao Te Ching

Consciousness is a gift. It gives us the ability to be here and, within that, the ability to feel the joy that emanates naturally from pure being. Consciousness represents our roots and the world, our nutrients. Rooting into the now means being present and remaining open to everything that moves from the vast background into the foreground before us. As stated above, the master of consciousness who is at one with himself is completely in tune with life. He wastes nothing. The honking car, the passing bird, the angry friend, the beleaguered family member, and the purring cat fuel his very existence. Her consciousness is a burning fire that feeds on the logs of her daily experiences. His being is effortless, his openness is infinite, and his deep roots provide connection – equanimity, balance, and wisdom. When one embodies awareness – taking in good and bad, dark and light, hard and easy, then life becomes an intimate experience. This is the final destination: *to embody the light of awareness* through raising our level of being, our level of consciousness. When the machine – the small egoic mind inside of us – churns, stop and ask, "human being or human doing?"

> Question: How rooted are we in the here and now? How open are we to receiving the nutrients flowing around us at all times?

Human being: our 'humanity' is the representation of our physical form, our earthly nature. 'Being' is consciousness, our ability to be aware of what occurs around us, and most importantly, within us. We are always human beings. What we are focusing on here is the degree to which we are beings. We want to raise our consciousness in order to enhance the experience we have and to touch beyond the confines of the fog we find ourselves in. Truly being requires turning inward.[36]

To describe living under the governorship of the ego, Buddha offers us the powerful image of a house on fire. Each time a flame is extinguished, another springs up, and so the cycle continues. Buddha refers to this repetitive pattern as one of delusional living. The issue is not the fire or the home, but rather it is our way of dealing with the situation. Instead of stopping, instead of looking deeply into ourselves to penetrate beyond the appearance of things, we constantly strive to douse the flames with explanations, defenses, habits, drugs, neuroses, and so forth. We say to others, "If only you did this, if only you took out the trash, if only you would stop, if only you would start…" This is an endless cycle. The buck always rests with us, and we must be the ones to take responsibility for ourselves.

Like the Buddha, the teaching is simple: turn your light of awareness – which is incessantly seeking outside – back in on yourself. Stop fighting the apparent flames coming in the guise of different surface-level appearances. Stop doing, the endless moving and shaking, and come back to the vibrant stillness of being.

On the surface of one's life lies the ego's constant struggle to maintain dominance. There is much more to life than finding ways to stay distracted. Begin by being honest with yourself about where you are in life. Become the watcher of your life on a moment-to-moment basis. Practice mindfulness and be aware of what you are doing, your level of being, and also, why you choose to do what you do.

There are deep insights to be had within this process. Watch and listen quietly and see what happens on its own. The world would be a far different place if there were seven billion human beings rather than doings. Again, ask yourself, *"Human being or Human doing?"*

Beware: Alienation & "The Dark Night of the Soul" [37]

Beware: walking the spiritual road, especially within the

context of western society, can at first seem a little daunting, if not alienating. When I first began to look into my life, change occurred and I could feel old versions of my personality falling by the wayside. The world I moved through was beautiful, but also a little distant, and I felt a need to push back against or judge what I was moving through. It was a bumpy road and I sometimes found myself falling out of love with the idea of not knowing who I was or what I thought about the person smoking a cigarette. It felt strange to think that I was different, to think that my changing didn't follow the tune of my surroundings.

Having small metaphorical funerals for the images I had created, and through which I had previously lived, gave rise to soulful moments. I could feel the lightness of transformation, but also the heaviness of watching an old friend, an old attachment, drift off into empty space. Like watching a burning pyre, stepping into the spiritual realm, the now, and letting go of old cherished habits and beliefs was painful.[38] It is very nice to read poems about lightness and the never-ending peaks of deep spirituality, but there is darkness too, ready and waiting for us to walk right into it to glean the deepest understandings.

If we have cultivated an image and we have propped up our egos over the years, we may have surrounded ourselves with people who are in the same boat, and who may not understand our sudden changing. Some of those may fade from our lives. But this newly acquired space, and our acceptance of this space, will open the doors for new meaningful relationships and experiences to come in and blossom. Trust this: trust space. More good and beautiful things come because we have changed our definition of what 'good' and 'beautiful' are. And, what if there is no definition? We may suddenly feel a new sense of freedom stemming from openness. Not having definitions may allow a quality of intimacy and connection with *this* life that we may have otherwise never experienced. We are expanding, becoming more open and able to see the keys to the door – the door to *this* life – buried within.

> It is from within the murkiness where the marrow of life can be extracted; it is within darkness that the light can be found. If you need evidence, *look into the night sky*.

Your ego, as it did with me, might question you.[39] In fact, as you begin to see more deeply into the nature of life, your mind may attempt to stop you or to think of ways to rationalize any space you create. The ego will do what it can to wriggle its way in, or to explain: doubts, emotional reactions, fears, false perceptions, assumptions, every tool the ego has at its disposal, will be employed for its defense, its survival. And in these repeated attempts, the ego will suddenly seem utterly insane to you. I repeat: the mind's incessant, selfish, and emotionally driven nature will seem absolutely small and insane. When you realize this fully, you will be ready to move more deeply and to go beyond your fictitious walls. It is not the world, or my family situation, or my social background that is the problem, it is my thoughts and my inability to inhabit the now. Leap into that and what else is there left to do? Transitioning to this view may be easy, but it also might bring out old demons that need to be recognized, experienced, and allowed to settle into the now with us.

The mind will do or think what it can to throw you off balance, to stop you from experiencing reality and depth. Through conditioning and following the images we have carefully created throughout our lives, the ego has become our master and commander and it will not relinquish its title without a struggle. So when you are questioning yourself while walking the path, know what is happening. This is part of the darkness and it leads to understanding. Be aware of what is taking place. Do not fight the mind and do not react. Rather, learn to embrace all stirrings. Slowly you will become the silent watcher and you will take the reigns of *this experience* into your own hands.

Witnessing *is* patience.

It takes effort, it takes mindfulness, it takes awareness, it takes faith in space, and it involves our total acceptance of the now and thus letting go of who we thought we were and our narrow view of reality. We fall and we get back up, but we are not alone. There are thousands of people who are on the path and many more who are suffering but do not know the depth of their being. There are people who might be stuck in their own life situation, their own conditionings, *because they know of nothing else.* It could be you. There are some who see more distractions, more television, more buying, more traveling, more partners, or more alcohol as the way to something fulfilling – continually feeding the hungry ghost. Have compassion for all people, including yourself, and know that the universe and the now hold us all moment-to-moment.

Remove yourself from the crashing waves of surface-level fulfillment. Rather than continually bashing and thrashing with the waves, dive under them. We are swimming out to sea to embody water. This is the metaphor. Swimming into the deep ocean. We need to break free from the shore break that has always thrashed us. To do this, we dive under the whitewater and we give all our effort to staying under while expanding outward. Initially it is difficult, but after a few waves, and with a little courage, it becomes easier and we wonder why we haven't done this before. We head out to sea, underneath the rolling swells. We go down and down, becoming calmer and more aware. It is an interesting place full of countless possibilities. Giants live here, our fears, our past, our demons live here too, waiting to be confronted and accepted when the time comes. But we are strong from the waves and we are realizing more and more that the encompassing ocean, in all its depth, vastness, glory, and wonder, is who we are. This insight *is* touching our core. It is no different from this.

In the end, we must be willing to become a conscious individual first and foremost for ourselves: it is our journey to experience, our road to walk. Do it for your Self. The power to become more conscious comes from within. Its source of inspiration and its intention must thus be from within as well. You will be empowered with this simple realization: it is your choice, your freedom, and your life.

What Lies Ahead

"The beginning of wisdom is found in doubting; by doubting we come to the question, and by seeking we may come upon the truth."

— Pierre Abelard

"The journey of one thousand miles begins with one step."

— Lao Tzu

On our journey, there are certain aspects – ways of being, movements of life, lessons to feel – that must be examined. Below, I have laid out some of the key words, contemplative states, and quotes that I explored and am still exploring on my inner journey. But let's begin by taking it to basics. Relax for a moment and think about who you are, using the phrase, "I am…" For example, "I am Rachel, I am 30 years old, I am a paralegal, I am tall, I am beautiful, I am a college graduate, I am an American…" All great information – everything one would bring up in a casual conversation. But right now you are alone and there is nobody watching, so it's ok to let go for a little experimentation. Now, what if you just stopped at, "I am." What if for one moment you let go of the name you were given, the college you went to, the political ideology or party with which you are affiliated and the cherished opinions you firmly stand by? Let it all go for a moment or two and see what washes away. In this moment, for the sake of practice, all you have is, "I AM." "I AM alive, I AM a being." "Right now I am going to be just that – free." This is freedom.

When we let go of everything we deem 'important,' when we step out of the bubble of conditioned existence and enter into the world of being, life takes on a new texture. We are removing the emphasis on "I" and thus getting rid of the need to compare, to judge, to remain a separate identity from an inherently interconnected existence. We are making room for being. Life is a little lighter, a little more real and vivid. There is more space for our energy to occupy being instead of constantly working to maintain an old image of who we think we are. And as a result, we are more *here*, tapping into our innate qualities. Nothing has

54

changed just our view and our energy level. We are more alive! We are less separated and more connected not only to ourselves, but to the world. The tree is greener and the sound of cars on the street comes in and out of our ears, not as the sound of rushing cars, but as pure sound. Through being – seeing, hearing, breathing, and feeling – become just as they are, without a commentary: straight, unfettered clarity is the result. There is nothing to cloud us from these simple treasures. And when we can move and behave in a way that reflects this inner stillness, we have purpose and we have a silent power. Less labeling of self automatically leads to less labeling of what is going on, and everything begins to unravel from there.

Being is a simplification in a way, but one that leads to profound depth and understanding – something that cannot be grasped by the thinking mind. The more letting go we do and the more grounded we are in what is happening in the here and now, the wiser and more in tune we are.[40] Conversely, the worldlier, the more complex, the more idiosyncratic, the more titled we are, and the more we define our lives by such things, the less we are truly living.

> Sitting with, "I Am" is just a small practice, something to make a little room for inner growth. Let it seep for a while.

The following chapters are comprised of practices, words, and advice for life on the path of mindfulness. Starting with Beyond Knowing, accepting the scope of inner examination and the non-intellectual nature of the process, we examine certain pieces, the gems of the road, that will help deepen our experience. Examining "Letting Go," "Space," "Surrender," "Equanimity," and "Impermanence" helps push us toward a greater understanding of being and what it means to live in the moment. Looking at each of these aspects deeply, we begin to learn more about our Selves and the universe that we move through, and which in turn moves through us. How to act, how to think, how to be, how to meditate, how to deepen, all need to be learned, practiced, and directly experienced. There is a long way to go and this is just the beginning. But, it isn't a no-sum game. There isn't a rule of, "enlightenment or bust!" For each step on its own brings more consciousness, more joy, and more unfettered reality.

> Despite the various descriptions of an awakening experience – sudden or gradual, religious or non-religious – the fundamental truth remains utterly clear: awakening is accessible within each passing moment… Like now… or now…

One's presence is the only paramount aspect – sitting comfortably on the edge of your nose and right above your brow. Wisdom, ethical living, and pure being naturally spring forth more and more. And we become our own compass, navigating with ease through whatever stands before us. This is living consciously. This is what it is all about. The treasures are here; we just need to reach down and *realize* their existence.

Everything before you is a kind of framework or even a diary of sorts, wrapped within a conversation. Take time to digest what you have read, and then let it settle for a while. The quotes, the words, the practices are part of my journey and they may unseat or release something within you. Trusting the process comes on its own from living the process. When we need to move we do so and when we need to stop and listen, we do so. The universe, through turning in, provides us with such insights.

There is darkness lurking somewhere in life as you already know. Light and dark, tragedy and comedy, and the interplay between the poles, is how we come to know happiness and intimacy with our moment-to-moment circumstances. Without the contrast between darkness and light, everything would be bland and unbearably dull. We would be living in a state of gray. Some of the chapter headings I chose uncovered darkness I did not know was there. It could be difficult or unpleasant to view, I would want to turn away and crawl back to the life of superficiality, shallow waves, and plastic coral reefs – to turn toward my explanations and my delusional refuges. But turning back from inner depth, from turning in, after everything I had felt and experienced, would have been to live in a dream knowing I was dreaming – a state of gray in its own way.

We are turning inward with the headlight of awareness firmly placed on our forehead, right above our eyes. Before us stands the cave and within the cave, gems faintly sparkle among the undeniable and hazy opaqueness surrounding the path. To get to the gems requires sincerity and patience. There is an impenetrable darkness and all we can perceive are the outlines of a faint pathway. But each gem we touch, each deepening, brings inner fortitude, wisdom and understanding. To be one's own master and to live a life that reflects this purity is the greatest gift. Deep consciousness and thus true experience are the goal.

> "Instead of blaming our discomfort on outer circumstances or on our own weakness, we can choose to stay present and awake to our experience, not rejecting it, not grasping it, not buying the stories that we relentlessly tell ourselves. This is priceless advice that addresses the true cause of suffering – yours, mine, and that of all living beings"
>
> – Pema Chodron, "Taking the Leap"

There are not many people in Western culture willing to open Pandora's box and peer into their own minds. This does not mean you shouldn't do so. Turning in on ourselves, we go deeper and deeper, peeling layer after layer to reach the core.[41] Sometimes there is pain behind unpeeling these layers because each layer does not want to lose its sway over us. The layers of our ego have become so ingrained that their removal hurts at first. They dissolve and what was once hidden within the layer is laid out naked in the open for us to view. Any pain we feel is a small funeral for those lost layers, and a reminder of the phantoms and baggage that have become visible. But in the morning – as always – comes the light and the sudden feeling of weightlessness. We have made more space for being. One ghost of our creation is gone – a deep opinion, an habitual pattern, a bad memory, a sore subject, reactive tendency, a long lost love has been cleared, and we have made more space for the innate qualities of our Self to fill the void naturally – opening the mind.

What you – I – we are doing, seeking a deeper understanding through turning in and witnessing, is a wonderful thing, though doubts will surely rise. Turning away from a life of ghosts and forms to find the inherent qualities within all of us is a noble process and a beautiful journey. We are changing the world by changing ourselves. That is how real, tangible change comes, *one conscious person at a time. You are what matters.*

Seekers are naturally deep people, but our culture is not entirely conducive to our aspirations. We know this, but we seek anyway because deepening far outweighs the other in profundity and substantiality. Our willingness to find ourselves in a society that has lost touch brings everything closer to striking a balance. You, embodying change, are the ultimate form of change.[42]

> "Just as treasures are uncovered from the earth, so virtue appears from good deeds, and wisdom appears from a pure and peaceful mind. To walk safely through the maze of human life, one needs the light of wisdom and the guidance of virtue"
>
> – Buddha

Meditation

"Not yet having entered the gate, nevertheless I have discerned the path"

— Ten Bulls

Meditation is the door to the inside, it is our avenue – our Broadway – for turning in. It is the only way to touch our true being. Closing our eyes, feeling the energy within the body, and following our breath, we open the door.

When we meditate, we are consciously and powerfully signaling to ourselves that we are here and that we are committed to understanding and knowing our inner Self. We are getting in touch. Each time we meditate, our roots grow deeper and deeper. We become calmer, more aware of what is occurring around us at all times. The hawk flies by, the ant scurries across the floor, and we notice it. These are little events, but our ability suddenly to perceive more and more around us throughout the day opens us up to the greater possibilities in life. With increased meditation and heightened awareness, such sights bring joy of their own accord. Our level of enjoyment grows. Small events – the primary fabric of our lives – become wonders and these wonders become the keys to unlock ourselves to further growth, further expansion.

On the inside, the emotion rises and we feel it completely. We are able to see that what rises within is just an emotion. We smile at this insight and we allow ourselves to flow with what comes. Then, we let it pass. We are deepening, moving away from the world of form and touching the background, the infinite possibilities, the state of being that is just being. Getting more and more in touch with our inner workings, we become increasingly stable. We are conscious of what is coming up, what comes in, and what goes out. We are more aware of what pushes our buttons and we see through it clearly. We are also more aware of our reactions to these stimuli and our tendency to run to some habitual response to cover up or to make us feel better. This may seem small, but it is not.

Wisdom comes from meditation and the meditative lifestyle. Being here, being open, touching the calm beneath the reactions and judgments allows the *meditator* naturally to become wiser. He or she is bonding with something beyond any intellectual pursuit, something far deeper than thinking that precisely reflects the flow of life – something that lies within the infinity of the *now*.

> Chao-chou asked Nan-chuan, "What is the Tao?"
> Nan-chuan said, "Everyday mind is the Tao."
> Chao-chou said, "How can I approach it?"
> Nan-chuan said, "The more you try to approach it, the farther away you'll be."
> "But if I don't get close, how can I understand it?"
> The Master said, "It's not a question of understanding or not understanding. Understanding is delusion; not understanding is indifference. But when you reach the unattainable Tao, it is like space, limitless and serene. Where is there room in it for yes and no?"[43]

Oftentimes we say, "I don't have enough time to get my work done, exercise, eat, and pick up groceries! How am I going to meditate? Sitting idly, what a waste of time!" This is completely understandable, especially in the context of our society (GO GO GO! Don't look inside! Keep adding more and more things! Don't look through the mirror to see beyond all the important exterior reflections!). And yet, we have the time. We have the presence of mind to look beyond this fallacy. What must first take place, though, is our opening to the possibility of what meditation can bring, and also our sincere effort in maintaining a daily practice. We have to get the ball rolling by experiencing the benefits, being open to them, and taking control of the mind. All it takes is ten minutes of sitting, breathing, and witnessing.[44]

When I first started meditating, I didn't believe in the process, let alone benefits, at all. I could barely keep still for three minutes, and if I did, I was often elsewhere, thinking about the various things to 'do' or 'get' later on in the day. Always looking ahead, always living out the past, always looking away, that was my life. Finding distractions, this is what many of us do. In meditation we come back to our Selves in this moment. A good idea may arise and we let it go in order to come back to ourselves. Thoughts, desires to watch television, snack, exercise, write, work (insert distraction) come up and we let them go. This is the practice.

Am I a true individual, am I even here in this moment? What was the point of it all if I was never truly here? Such questioning humbled me. There is something separate, something much deeper than these pursuits. Going somewhere or reaching for something else was not the answer. We can spend our entire lives looking outwards and we will not find anything other than more searching. A famous Buddhist question facing young practitioners is, "When was the best day of your life?" Naturally, the practitioner thinks that it has not come yet. Well, what if it has? The bottom line is that each and every day is the best when we are able to tune in fully to what is happening – when we are present, aware of the movements within and without. What is… is.

I wanted to get in touch with who I am right here, right now. I wanted to sift through the soil to find what lay buried beneath. I had looked outwards for more – bigger, better, faster things and experiences, only to have each pass by, leaving me in the trough, waiting for the next thing to attach myself to. Meditation was a counterintuitive move. It seemed boring, unappealing, and on the surface, easy. My mind wanted nothing to do with it. *That was the key*. The fact that my mind, my controller – the black snake – feared such a way of life was what turned me inward in the first place.

As I said earlier, it was initially difficult to sit and stay motivated each and every day. Thoughts flowed through me, ideas sprang up, random obligations I had no intention of fulfilling tried to dissuade me – this was all further proof of the 'rightness' of meditation. It was a technique the mind feared because it was unable to be the controller in such an environment. It struggled and it writhed, but with time and effort, the struggling began to fade. After one week, meditation became easier. One week and the benefits began to appear. One week and I began to venture beyond the enclosed boundaries of who I thought I was: I became a little more conscious, a little more aware, and thus, more alive. You have everything to lose and nothing to gain in meditation. Letting go of the ramparts holding together my ego, inverting them and seeing them for what they were – the very walls of who I thought I was – was all that was necessary for me to create a hole to peer through, to feel the texture of being ok with whatever leapt out of infinity.

Meditation brings about a fundamental switch in the mind and body. Nothing happens; we still have our lovers, our jobs, our commitments, but now we begin to have our Selves. We are free, ideas and conceptualizations don't stick – there is no story or narrative to follow. And in knowing the Self, going deeper and deeper, we live more fruitful lives. We prune away the unnecessary, we become streamlined and we flow with the natural currents within the river of being.

Realizing how out of touch we are is the first step because when we see this, we are ready to give some real effort to our meditation practice. It is a humbling feeling to come to the realization that we lead lives that are often deadening and unconscious. But it is also a miracle to behold. In seeing, we have the opportunity to stop our old patterns and to begin anew, fresh with energy and vibrant consciousness. Any roadblocks we perceive are mental ones that we have created. It takes courage to overcome these mental projections the right way – through turning in and raising our awareness of what is. Finding the time and making the necessary space for cultivating a solid meditation practice is the next step. A quiet environment is essential for beginners. The mind will be hard enough to tame. Find a space where you can truly unravel and focus on being. Internally, let go of everything. Reflect the quiet environment you have found by releasing any worries or mental projections. Relax and be, but pay attention and be alert. We are working on letting go, being, but also on becoming more aware. Raising our consciousness means staying 'alive' as much as we can throughout our lives. There is a passionate alertness that runs hand in hand with the rising calm. Meditation is the door to realizing this and it is only kept open through daily practice. Removing the walls, opening the windows, taking down barriers, making space – this is the imagery. Keeping these avenues open and allowing the fresh breeze to come in, to cleanse, and to refresh each arising moment is the practice.

> "A Student of Tendai, a philosophical school of Buddhism, came to the Zen abode of Gasan as a pupil. When he was departing a few years later, Gasan warned him: "studying the truth speculatively is useful as a way of collecting preaching material. But remember that unless you meditate constantly your light of truth may go out."[45]
> - Your Light May Go Out, 101 Zen Stories, 52

Though we are just beginning, our goal is to bring meditation into our day. We want to touch this lucid awareness not just in our quiet space, but in the world we live in. We want to become *Beacons* – deep individuals, living in this world consciously, twenty-four seven. Our seated meditation practice lays the foundation. Each time we meditate, we signal to ourselves that we wish to uncover who or what we are at our core. What we uncover and touch in our meditative practice moves from the seated position out into our moving, fluid lives. Walking, working, running, laughing, crying, we begin to 'do' these activities consciously. The silent watcher is coming forth.

Here are some basic steps to getting started. If you meditate for fifteen minutes a day, seven days straight, meditation will show itself to you.

1. *Sitting, relaxing, centering* – Letting go, we are here, alive! It is time to let go of the day, of the ego, of our thoughts. It's time

to get in touch with the inner stillness below all these things. Our inner nature is right there, right below the surface. We are centered in an upright position, and we are deepening through letting go and being.

2. *Breathing – in, and then, out – focusing on the in and out of our breath –* This is our device, our tool. When we get flustered or bored, we can always return to the breath. It is our base – we cannot exist without it. Send a little thankfulness to the breath and return to it. There is nothing else to do but breathe and be. Paying attention to the breath allows us to focus on the body and thus disassociate ourselves from thoughts.

3. *Posture – Straight back, wide chest, drawn in stomach, aligned body, centered and sturdy, unshakable, rooted to the floor –* When we meditate we become an antenna for all that is. To receive, we must be aligned and rooted into the floor. Whether we are sitting on a chair or on a cushion makes no difference. A mountain is a mountain. We want to get the best energy flow possible. Remember, 'Deep roots and a mind like sky.' Buddhism and Hinduism teach the seven chakras or energy centers, which include: the crown, the brow, the throat, the heart, the solar plexus, the sacrum, and the base. When we meditate, we want to make sure that these seven energy centers are aligned. We want to promote flow within. Align yourself and flow…

4. *Remaining focused, concentrated on being right here, right now –*

Thoughts come, the mind is very busy and we are just beginning. Let the thoughts come, for they will be there. There is no need to be frustrated. Just come back to the breath and re-focus on the breath. We are here to be here. BOOM another thought comes and we attach. No problem, refocus and come back to the breath. Over and over we do this. It may take a week or two, but the mind will begin to still and slowly you will notice. Keep going, stay concentrated, without self-criticism, relaxed.

5. *Deepening inwardly and settling into this* – As we settle into our meditation, thoughts flow as waves flow across the vast ocean. We are the ocean and the thoughts are just small surface phenomena – a natural part of the ocean but nothing compared to the ocean's vastness and depth. These thought waves, no matter how large – twenty, thirty, maybe even fifty feet high, are nothing when they are placed against such a large background. This is the metaphorical imagery: the largeness, the ocean, the sky, or the mountain, remain unmoved by the small surface events. In reality, we are the ones who attach and who allow the small surface events to affect us. Sincere meditation puts an end to this. When we embody the inner ocean, the wave or cloud, the thought, the feeling, the emotion – floats by. We may feel it for a moment, but it has no bearing on our fundamental nature, and we let it pass; balanced, in touch, we remain.

I often liked to imagine jumping into a turbulent sea and sinking way down to the bottom. I would find a nice sea cave and sit at its mouth in peace. The turbulent ocean, full of thoughts and feelings was hectic, and yet I sat unmoved, completely still. A giant, fifty-foot wave would pass (thought: receiving a parking ticket), but from my vantage point it was barely visible. In fact, it was beautiful – a powerful wave moving across my internal ocean. Without attaching to it, it passed and I would remain alert, watching. Another thought (when am I going to get in my exercise today?) passes, a solid thirty footer, but once again, I witnessed, smiled and let it pass. Wow, this is consciousness, this is a beautiful thing. Learn to meditate and tame the wild seas, not by ending and controlling the storms, a notion that is a mere illusion of the ego, but by simply becoming the vast sea.

When you put these steps together and practice sincerely, meditation becomes something amazing. It gives back so much more than the time you put into it because it is giving you real life and true freedom. Changing your view, changing your level of being – turning in – enriches life. We become present, mindful of our feelings, and much, much more balanced. We are deepening our roots and getting in touch with the inner stillness. With effort and continued steady practice, our meditative state expands into our daily lives. Something giant, a huge wave comes. But we are a little more of the ocean this time around. The wave passes ferociously, but it passes. We enjoyed it a little bit, we noticed the aqua-blue tint of the wave as it reared up and heaved forward, the sun shimmering through the awesome spray and the relative warmth and liveliness of the surface-level water. We even took a small lesson from it as it went by. And we were barely moved by it because we had become the ocean, the water: the wave moved right through us without us moving, reacting or being affected. The wave was just a wave, and its sway over us depended only on how much our minds attached to it. Meditating, touching the deep ocean, cuts the mind out. What comes, comes, and we are here for it completely. As we deepen from this point and we begin to see reality, the waves have less and less of an effect.

As we continue to practice, we strive to live life in a meditative way: mindful and completely in tune with the present moment. Our minds cling and grasp at less and less. They resemble the sky more and more. We root deeper and deeper into the innate qualities of the Self, our heart-mind. There is no other way that brings more peace, more balance, and more understanding than meditation. Not only do we learn about ourselves, we learn about the movement of life. Acceptance and watchfulness arise.

"The world is ruled by letting things take their course."
- Lao Tzu

There are many guides for you to follow. Meditation is not someone else's tool, it is your own. You are the meditator and you will learn to do it in your own way as you progress. Be open to what it can bring and read further into the topic. There are also many audio recordings you can listen to that will ease the process. They will show you the various forms in which to meditate. Listen, incorporate, and then let go. Take the reins and silently, effortlessly turn in and experience truly who you are at your core. Touch the inner stillness, and let it come forth.

Beyond Knowing

"In the sky, there is no distinction of east and west; people create distinctions out of their own minds and then believe them to be true."

- Buddha

"Look, and it can't be seen. Listen, and it can't be heard... You can't know it, but you can be it, at ease in your own life. Just realize where you come from: this is the essence of wisdom."

- Tao Te Ching

"Understanding means throwing away your knowledge."
- Thich Nhat Hanh

As we begin to view the path, we realize that things are indeed out of our control and that what comes does so in a way that reflects the natural, shifting flow of life. In meditation, wisdom and insight appear of their own accord, without a 'how' or a 'why' attached to them. A series of feelings and images settles. There is more space around the things that enter into and step out of our lives. Internally, things begin to shift and we open up to dimensions of being that we could not have understood or experienced before. It's not that life is changing on an external level, but rather, I – you – we are changing ourselves. We are going into a region that is beyond knowing.[46]

I remember beginning to let go of who I thought I was in meditation, and having a sense of spaciousness permeate my daily experience: during strolls around the park, while jumping into the Pacific Ocean, in walking miles and miles through snow-capped mountains and down long ridges. It was as if a barrier had been lifted between the world and me, and there was a sudden meeting of sorts between the two of us. I could feel the calm spaciousness reverberating through the last streaks of sunlight on a warm evening, or out of the palm of a waving hand, and these instances had an effect on my opening. Putting down my mind, there wasn't anything to know in those moments. I had nothing to guard against or to believe in, and I began to feel a sense of freedom that came with the territory of letting go of knowing, my opinions, and my judgments.[47] These experiences laid a foundation for me to expand outwards, to bring a sense of openness into the sticky arena of family disputes, critiques, successes, and failures. With practice, I found it interesting to enter into realms I deemed uncomfortable, being ok with the fact that I was uncomfortable, and that everything was perfect the way it was. There wasn't any reason for it to be un-perfect other than the observation that my mind did not approve, and that I was fighting against the inevitable moment. I noticed how I would think up ways to get out of a situation or to react defensively, but when I didn't know – when I didn't have a prescribed vision of how things should be – I saw the comedy behind such cyclical behavior. In not knowing who I was or how or why things were, there was a weightlessness that allowed me to flow with the moment and greet the world intimately.

> "Sickness and medicine correspond to each other. The whole world is medicine. What am I?
>
> – Zen Master Yunmen

What am I? It seemed that my knowing, my trying to have an idea about how things should be, was the very barrier or affliction that prevented me from experiencing an inherent sense of connection to what is.

And the notion of knowing twists into more complex emotional realms, into what we force, rationalize, and falsely support. I often found myself being 'ok' with moments that weren't ok for me. I would don social masks or force something without deeply accepting it. I would pretend to know. There was some rigidity in these moments and I could feel it in my body. When I brought Bodhidharma's "I don't know" into these moments, I found that I had been suppressing a great deal of pain, pretending that things were 'fine,' to conform with what I thought was bearable and necessary – the same fundamental logic that keeps lovers locked in physically abusive relationships, children tight-lipped over past incidents, and religious fanatics' congealed and hardened opinions unshaken.[48] And this way of thinking manifested itself in my created world. What I knew and thus how I thought the world should be, fed a perpetual state of conflict between reality and my little view of the world. Practicing not knowing and acceptance of the present might remove this subtle conflict within the mind and allow it to expand into *this*.

Not knowing then isn't rigid and intellectually based on one side or languid and blasé on the other because there *are* no sides or distinctions. All that is left is this moment as it is.[49] Spiritually, going beyond knowing is openness that forgets it is even open – it is just empty space. Learning how to bring this natural, accepting behavior into our daily lives is a key element for our path.

Here are some basic points to remember throughout the day. These principles bring us back to being. And 'to be' means to go beyond the known, the confines of the ego – to see the mental cages we create.

The goal: Consciousness – touching the inner Self, and thus, no goal

The Way: turning in, witnessing

The teachers: Buddha, the Masters, and many others

The ultimate truths: You are the way. Follow intently but then let go.

Getting in touch with, or embodying the Self through turning in, has much less to do with the small mind than what lies beneath it. We are working on uncovering our Selves. We are the goal, and at the same time, we are the path. They are one in the same, and the steps above, at some point, fold into each other. The process – walking the path – means transcending the mind. There isn't an intellectual blueprint that involves trying or striving, but a natural one grounded in letting go.[50] This seems slightly counterintuitive, and it is. We are getting in touch with our true nature, what is already present and constant, our essence. Our nature, pure being, requires getting down to the basics, that which feels simple, peaceful, balanced, and leads to 'oneness.' Essentially, what is already right *here*.

As I said earlier, we do not need a Ph.D. for turning in. In fact, the less logic, the easier the process. It is very important to understand this deeply. The Buddha, though profoundly enlightened, was a human being like you and me. He stepped away, he saw through, and he laid down a path for seekers to walk upon into their own minds. His methods were at first extreme – starvation, nihilism, pain, transcendence – but it was not until he sat under a Bodhi tree and faced himself, intimately touching the earth, that he became enlightened. After seeing through his trials and tribulations and letting go of striving, the Buddha was able to show the world the power and the peace of mind that lie inherently within every human.[51] Few tap into this power, but it can never be taken away from us if we choose to embody it. We can work at lessening suffering and bringing light into the world just by becoming more conscious of ourselves – our actions, our thoughts, our speech – and in the end, by cultivating mindfulness. Turning in, we discern the path toward higher consciousness. The more conscious and aware we become, the more we can move beyond and transcend the boundaries and limits we put on ourselves.

Nan-in illustrated this point in the Zen story called, "A Cup of Tea."

> Nan-in, a Japanese master during the Meiji era (1868-1912), received a university professor who came to inquire about Zen. Nan-in served tea. He poured his visitor's cup full, and then kept pouring.
> The professor watched the overflow until he no longer could restrain himself. "It is overfull. No more "will go in!"
>
> "Like this cup," Nan-in said, "you are full of your own opinions and speculations. How can I show you Zen unless you first empty your cup?"
>
> - 101 Zen Stories, 1

Too much mind, too much logic, too much worldliness, too much heaviness, too many problems, too much praise, too many distinctions and definitions, stand in the way of inner truth – truth that is innate and beyond any conceptualization of the mind. When we remove mental barriers, wisdom naturally appears and it comes in the form of being – not doing, thinking, proving. It is already naturally here! With our logic come doubt, judgment, reaction, and argument. Duality, defensiveness, disconnection, and separation become their byproducts. Remember, we have an ego and we believe that it must be defended at all costs! This is where all suffering lies, where things need to be a certain way or else, where we defend 'who' we think we are – our created small self. Going beyond this, going beyond the mind and reaching for a deeper level, we learn to be in this world, but not completely of it. We learn to maintain balance, we learn to go beyond knowing and to be comfortable with ourselves as we tread the territory of an unknown wilderness.

The egoic mind is all about doing, thinking, striving. It thinks incessantly and this constant stream of thoughts keeps one from pure being. Within unadulterated being, which is a state that lies beyond the mind, beyond knowledge, resides our innate Self. To touch this, we must inhabit the present moment, devoid of our issues, problems, thoughts, and nagging dilemmas. It is that simple and that challenging! Learn and practice just to be, here and now.[52] Unpeel the layers of mind and deepen on an unimaginable scale. If this seems difficult to understand or if it is hard to accept, don't worry, it is supposed to ruffle some feathers. We are learning to pluck the mind. Through recognizing our thoughts and opinions as unnecessary obstacles, we separate ourselves from who or what we think we are, providing an opportunity for an inner transformation. This also allows us to see the path for what it is: a process that relies on feeling and being rather than intellectual pursuit. Yes, there is effort, there is sincerity, there is learning, but it is all headed toward less mind and more pure, conscious being.

Going for the natural: learn to be still or at least to be ok with stillness. There is pure consciousness – who or what you are

– inhabiting this space. When we come to know this place, the small things fall by the wayside.

Though others have walked the path and can describe it, their experience is their own. Turning in is your own activity. *Through you is You.* We are not trying to idolize or be somebody else, this is to be driven off course. Buddha was very adamant about this point. He continually told his disciples not to get too attached to Dharma teachings or phrases. This lesson was the illustration of Buddha. For hundreds of years after his death, Buddha was signified as footsteps in the sand. That was his symbol. Just footsteps. "I am nothing," said he. See the incredible meaning behind this. Don't idolize me. Don't get distracted by me – know thy Self! A famous Zen master echoed Buddha's ancient and profound wisdom when he later said:

"If you see the Buddha on the path, kill him!"

Looking deeply we see the truth behind this declaration. The Zen master's evocative words cut right to the core of turning in. "Kill the Buddha," means follow your heart, follow heart-mind. Don't let anything or anyone distract you. Don't get caught up in following others, the opinions of others, or even your own opinions and thoughts. There is no need. Buddha is there as a tool for us – as a raft to reach the other shore.[53] His teachings are tools for us to use. Don't idolize these tools, use them, says the Zen master. Unpeeling layer after layer, we make our way inward. With each layer come balance, wisdom, and clear vision, all innate qualities within us.[54]

Buddha's way, the Dharma, is a road map for us to use. Follow the steps diligently. Let them seep into your budding practice. But then we let go of them. We still practice mindfulness, awareness, concentration and acceptance of what is, but it is our mantra, not the Buddha's or anyone else's. We pay our respects to the ancient masters and sages. We thank them for pointing us toward the Way, we have deep gratitude for their compassion in sharing their wisdom, risking their lives through political and religious turmoil for our well-being. But then we return to our practice, ourselves. For if we miss this point, if we let the moment go by without seeing through, we never claim ourselves and we become stuck in yet another perpetuated cycle. Buddhism, Christianity – any religion or teaching – can become its own self-serving attachment. Religion or philosophy becomes something we identify with, something we follow for comfort. There are beautiful, descriptive roadmaps to inner peace, but they are not the answer alone: they are just descriptions that only come to life through our direct experience. If you truly believe that getting in touch with the Self is the goal, and that you are the path, then why not accept this fully?

Being your Self means letting go of conceptualization and rationalization. The more logical we are, the farther from the Self we are. This is strange to grasp at first, but that is ok. Once we grasp it, we let go. This is when we realize the state of beyond knowing. It, life, us, where we are at this moment, just is.

It all seems so simple. Below the surface, I am Buddha. There is absolute truth to this statement. It is right here, clear as day. And yet we are unable to touch it. We can't envision such an existence because we see it as separate from our own experience.[55] Overcoming our limitations, working with the rational and irrational, and letting go of our opinions and distinctions help us create an open state of mind. Letting go of the mind and focusing on being, as much as possible, is how we set our base. Just be the witness.[56]

> Nan-ch'üan asks Tao-wu, "What can you say about that place that knowledge does not reach?"
>
> Tao-wu replied, "One should absolutely avoid talking about that."
>
> Nan-ch'üan said, "Truly, as soon as one explains, horns sprout on one's head, and one becomes a beast!"

Space

"In all chaos there is a cosmos, in all disorder a secret order."
- Carl Jung

"I think about that "empty" space a lot. That emptiness is what allows for something to actually evolve in a natural way. I've had to learn that over the years – because one of the traps of being an artist is to always want to be creating, always wanting to produce."
- Meredith Monk

What if things happened naturally, out of nothing, out of nowhere, like the Big Bang, or a sudden creative idea? What if making space and consciously being at ease in the space we inhabit was an avenue for us to experience a deeper understanding? It is a magical idea that isn't magic at all. It only appears to be magic to those of us who have remained out of touch with the internal.

Space is the infinite background that allows all things – without discrimination – to be, to change, to thrive, to move, and to transform.

We often take space for granted. In western culture, space is the emptiness that produces nothing. Haven't you heard the saying, "nothing comes from nothing?" In the modern world and the modern mind, space must be filled with objects, thoughts, statistics, and other various adornments. We think that we have to do something in order for things to happen. This belief, which lies at the core of our society, could not be farther from the natural truth – the truth that stretches back farther than modern human history, deep into the recesses of geological time and beyond. By just being, remaining clear and unclouded, the world greets us on its own accord. Dropping doing, manipulation, stress, resistance, reaction, judgment – all the products that cloud space – and entering into conscious emptiness, we create the space necessary for growing, for sprouting. It is that simple.

In present-day life, most of us are so obsessed with doing that we lose touch with being. Everything becomes something to do and our fluttered, flustered, time-consuming lives reflect this robotic mechanization. When we lose touch with being, life becomes a fight and we are forced to resist the natural flow, and to be out of the flow, to be out of being, means living a life of resistance. These clouds keep us from knowing our inner depth, our true nature: the clear awareness known as the Self. We can reverse this trend by simply making more space throughout our cluttered day. Looking around and seeing things as they are, without judgment or labeling, is a good practice. Placing ourselves in whatever is happening without clutching or without being somewhere else – just being right here, right now can lead to an opening. Even focusing on the space around objects might blow down a barrier within.

Space is a frightening concept for the small mind because it implies emptiness. We believe that emptiness is negative, dead or even a waste. It is undone, it is stale, and it represents the unknown wilderness beyond the confines of our mental maps. Nothing for the ego to grapple with implies ego's demise. When confronted by space, the small mind often works to fill it up with thoughts, preoccupations, schedules, emotions, drinks, fantasies, anything that we can imagine or physically get our hands on. If you imagine an empty house, you immediately begin to designate rooms, to label them and to fill each room: the master bedroom, the kitchen, the entertainment room, with various colorful objects, televisions, couches, and lamps. You paint the walls and you turn on the lights. "Ah," you say, "much better." Using your creative mind to build a house isn't a bad thing, but what I want you to look at here is the compulsion to fill space. What pushes us to fill space, to deny a natural emptiness?

84

Now change the metaphor of the house into the mind. Is there space in the mind, and if so, do you allow it to be as it is? Is there room for change, for your Self? What about life? When there is something 'wrong,' or when we are down, do we allow space? Do we greet the moment as it is and allow it to settle? Not usually. What if the answer to our problems comes from the emptiness we make instead of a forced and fundamentally reactive solution? By this I mean what if we allow what *is*, right here, right now, just to be? And, what if we create space? Rather than going after the answer, through space, the answer comes to us.[57] Are we open to this? Nothing, space, emptiness is the hallmark of a blank canvas. When we let things be (the sadness, the question, the moment), without knowing, the answer or some course of action often appears out of thin air. If we are open and spacious, putting down our prescribed likes and dislikes, then the naturalness, the 'thusness' of the answer becomes apparent.

Within space and emptiness resides the Self. Your potential realization of the true Self is the reason why the small mind incessantly runs day after day. It is trying to stay alive, trying to stay useful and relevant to you. It needs to project the next thing for you to focus on and it needs you to buy into it completely. It must see people looking down on you and it must take things personally, striving for the next thing or opinion to behold. It is the cyclical nature of the small mind, keeping us on a treadmill for life. You will reach and grasp because your small mind, is afraid of stepping into empty, wide-open space.

We fill space with things because it is comfortable and it is what we are used to doing. Remember, we are often defined by externalities, possessions, and titles because we live in a culture that emphasizes such things. When we step into the vastness of the background and embody the empty nature of space, externalities lose their grip. The symptoms of our disconnection from a deeper reality become illuminated by the light of our awareness. Our neuroses, our compulsions, and our suffering, in a sense, come from our fear of space, stillness, the *unknown, and the uncontrollable.* The more we unconsciously clutter our lives with fleeting externalities the less happy and fulfilled we will be because we are inhabiting an illusion.

> Technology is a wonderful thing, there is absolutely no doubting or refuting this. It has saved countless lives while connecting the global community on an unimaginable scale. However, on a deeper level, technology is filling our internal space. It is a new way for us to clutter, for us to hide from true meaning – to keep busy. The gadget, the cell phone, the wireless internet, the games, the television, can become means for us to fill space and to escape the present. Escaping from the present further alienates us from our Self. We become increasingly egocentric, unable to see the vastness of reality – we are cut off from living a realized life. Our hiding, coupled with our armored state of being, completely sterilize us from a deeper intimacy.

Space is an essential ingredient for life. Without space, nothing grows. It is a necessary requirement for our lives to manifest. Make sure you consciously and respectfully make space for life: A garden of space for the moment to unfurl and bestow its gifts. If you give it space and you give it faith, what comes, comes, and the doors of the mind are open to the possibilities. Learn to cherish and love space. When you meditate, create space within. Let the space be on its own without any interference. With continued awareness you will appreciate what comes of its own accord. With time, you will be amazed at the number of opportunities that pass through your cultivated space. It will become a garden that replenishes itself and is welcoming to the arriving guest, the darkness, and the passing breeze.

> Sit and be still.
> See what is really there in front of you, to what you are completely oblivious. Put the phone down and just be. Put your thoughts down. Relax. Put this book down and just be… see space for your Self.

What was that like? Were you able to sit with the openness of the now – with what is actually happening in this moment? Were you able to see the clutter within the mind? If not, try again. Read this page again and then be for a moment. This is very important because it will create a small bubble of consciousness on which you will be able to build. Try to experience this as many times as you can during your busy day. Allow space whenever possible. Allow space to come in and let it expand. Creating space will bring peace of mind and it will give you a deeper understanding of life. Focus on being for being's sake, for the sake of your life and the lives of others with whom you come into contact.

Faith

"When students in this modern world fail to make progress, what's the problem? The problem is they *don't have faith in themselves*. If you don't have faith in yourself then you will be forever in a hurry trying to keep up with everything around you. You'll be twisted and turned in whatever environment you are in... But if you can just stop this mind that goes rushing around moment-by-moment looking for something, then you'll be no different than the ancestors and Buddhas. Would you like to get to know the ancestors and Buddhas? They are none other than you, the people in front of me, listening to this lecture on the Dharma."

– Master Lin-chi (d. *867* AD)

Coinciding with space is faith. To move openly through space and to trust in the freedom that comes with space, we must have faith in ourselves: faith to be at peace with the moment, to root into ourselves, to embody the ocean without being rolled around in the waves. For me, having faith in myself meant being ok with what was happening. In Buddhism, there is often the image of a wild horse, ox, or monkey that must be found in the wild first, and then tamed over time. This wild animal was none other than my own mind, "rushing around moment-by-moment looking for something" outside of my Self and the present moment. As I continued to search outside, I couldn't find what I was looking for. Maybe I thought I needed to get drunk and have a wild time. Maybe I needed to go into the mountains for a day, or maybe I was looking for a juicy hamburger to sink my teeth into. It didn't matter because all these quick fixes led me in the opposite direction – out and away.

Master Lin-chi's quote opened up an avenue for me: I couldn't remain open to *this* life without having faith in my Self, without knowing that *this* life would unfold and continue to unfold, and that I would experience it as it came and went. When I didn't have faith in my Self, I would drift off into thought, I would worry, I would project, I would try to control, and I would start to see contentment as something that came with striving for things that were outside of *this* moment, *this* body, and *this* experience.

I remember sitting by my desk while I finished a paper proposal. I saw waves of papers, issues, life and death, old memories, births, weddings, and distant challenges looming through my computer screen and out onto the horizon twisting into my mind. I felt stressed and lonely. I began to doubt the things I had done and the things that had not even occurred yet. Flowing with these thoughts down onto the floor and closing my eyes, Lin-chi's words appeared. In that moment I realized that I had abandoned myself. I had forgotten about *this* life. There wasn't anything profound about recalling the master's words, or the Buddhas and ancestors that floated through the letters, just an intimate understanding. Coming back to the moment and dropping into my body, I returned to my seat and I began to write. It was a simple move, an acknowledgment of the inherent freedom and depth within the now, which brought me back, not an explosion of feeling, a rigorous defense, or a consoling justification of whether I was right or wrong. There was just a conscious remembrance,

"Oh yeah, here I am, taming the wild ox and leading him through the shifting terrain of life."

This maneuver can seem dull to those of us who expect lights, fireworks, and entertainment. But the remarkable thing is, having an experience of sitting in the present during an ordinary moment and having faith in our Selves is all that is needed for a profound change of heart and mind to occur. In an instant, life comes forth and who we thought we were fades, just as a figment of imagination falls into the sudden awareness of an awakened dreamer. "Wake up!" All I can say to myself and to you is, have faith in your Self. When we calm our minds and come back to *this* life in the midst of infinity, there is a freedom that can hold us intimately through any storm.[58] A contemporary Zen teacher in northern California asks, "When you fall you fall, but how do you fall out of the infinite universe?" In the same way, I ask, "How do you fall out of the all-encompassing Self?" They are one in the same.

When we are able to create space and when we come to the realization that things, no matter how big or small, manifest on their own, without our meddling, our controlling, then we can have a little fun with it. Life is not all serious business. It is not all about nothing, everything, the universe, God, contemplation, meditation, success, failure, etc. We are living in the here and now in the midst of infinity. We are an increasingly conscious being, attempting to see through our conditioned existence – going against everything that has been placed upon us and that we have spent so much time and effort holding together, time spent outside of our Selves.

Faith then, is placing trust in your Self – knowing that the fruits of the spiritual Way will manifest as you continue to deepen. It is also trust grounded deeply in the mystery within the wilderness of the universe.[59]

Leaving the shore of form and moving out into the unknown is not easy. One must possess a level of faith in the Self deep enough to move beyond the hurdles of desire, fear, doubt, ego, and attachment, to trust change – to be ok with impermanence – to fall head first into the unknown – and eventually, to deeply accept the connections contained within it all.

Some pillars that might be a good starting point:

1. *The Core* – Mindfulness, awareness, concentration, and acceptance of what is.

2. *The View* – The universe is an infinite interconnected web and I am part of it. I am an inter-being and I will live in a way that reflects this.

3. *The Wisdom* – Life is impermanent. I too will leave my body. Energy is constant, it never dies – it only changes. I am energy.

4. *The Presence* – The only moment is now. Being is all there is. I am right here, right now. "Oh yes, here I am. Come on ox."

These principles, or something very close to them, could be your anchor, your refuge, and your source of inner fortitude through the journey of deepening. As long as you can remain in contact with these elements, faith will be there. You can't fall out of the universe or the Self. If you do, it is just the small mind pulling and tugging you back into the cave and the fog. If you wish, keep these principles close, merge with them and become them. This is truly it, right now. Enjoy the direct experience of now and know the ultimate reality we move through. You can have a very deep relationship with life when you are able to cultivate faith in your Self. Let go and leap – *gracefully* – into the whole.

Spontaneity

"Kindness and wildness is a poignant combination"

- John Tarrant

"What is it!"

- Master Ma-Tsu

How do you go about your daily business? Do you have a tendency to plan excessively? Do you find it necessary to control what is happening in your immediate vicinity? Can you let things be? Do you trust your innate intuition? Do you project your thoughts onto life or follow a subjective narration of how things are? Where are you right now? These are interesting questions to ask ourselves because each question sheds light on how much faith we have in our natural way and the natural way of the world around us. It's good to catch ourselves in our delusions sometimes, to see how easily we fall into our own subjective worlds, losing sight of the vastness of the now and the ultimate sense of freedom that accompanies the spacious and open mind. If joy and balance come from nowhere, then maybe we can trust this nothingness to guide our actions on the path, whether while buying groceries, driving to work, or speaking to a loved one over previously ignored grievances. Spontaneity, then, is action that flows with what is happening now. It isn't forced and controlled, or shallow and indifferent. Devoid of constraints, thoughts, or projections, spontaneous action is action that flows with the current.

> Going with the river of life means placing faith in the here and now – the one happening this moment – and letting go, allowing action to unfold naturally without any accompanying explanations.[60]

When we are able to let go, life greets us. Even the seemingly mundane moments and objects we move through have a quality to them that shines silently. There isn't a need to fight anymore or a sense of heaviness. Within spontaneity, there is a transparency that our own mind embodies. Life becomes a miracle and we are completely in tune with it. Like a beautiful, melodious song, or better yet, a dance partner, one can simply begin to move naturally with what comes and goes, whether it appears as a slow dance in the grade school gymnasium, or a Polynesian fire dance before an evening deluge of rain. Trusting in life, trusting in space, and having faith in letting go inevitably lead to trusting our inner Self. We don't waste energy propping up a fictitious reality. When we remove the exterior and give space for the interior to come forth, spontaneous action becomes a real possibility. It's not that the seas part, or that a mysterious figure from the sky comes down, it is *you* – expanded into *this* life.[61] What else is there?

Action that flows with the current of the now stems from an open mind that suddenly isn't constrained by anything. Sometimes we don't even notice it and other times, we feel a sudden transformation. The only way I can describe spontaneity without blasting it to pieces is through a kind of personal illustration of the latter:

The earth shook, or so my mind thought it did. But it hadn't. The moment was a very ordinary one. All that had changed was my previous view of the world and how I experienced the now, with fresh eyes and an open mind. There was an intimacy, a feeling of the texture of the world around me, pulsating into what I was stepping through right now, without having any idea of who I was or why I was taking part in some motion swirling outside my skin.

Spontaneous action showed itself to me in the middle of domestic arguments: being stuck in whether or not I was right, suddenly reaching out to my partner to ask how her work was going. It also leapt out while telling authority figures that they had gone too far, or while crossing the street to put coins in an old homeless man's cup. A merging of the mind and the world I moved through also meant I could feel an inherent sense of connection to what was here – stemming from the edge of moist fern leaves and just reaching out to touch their unfurling green tendrils. These weren't "aha" moments. They were natural and they came without thought, logic, or premeditation. Not dwelling on the actions, they passed naturally into the past and I moved into the next moment. It was interesting to notice that the more I moved with these motions without knowing why I was doing what I was doing, the more real and alive everything seemed. All that was there was the narrative-less moment.

As discussed earlier, things happen out of nothingness. It is an amazing thing to witness. One who observes life and who remains completely alert through the practice of vigilant awareness experiences a 'thusness' there, time and time again. We also see that thoughts and ideas come to us as well, from nowhere. Many of these thoughts are rebuffed by the mind or caught in the stickiness of what we subjectively want to pay attention to. The mind stands as a barrier between us and unencumbered action. As we continue to unpeel, natural movement will surface. We are getting in touch with the creative part of you – the inner part of you that does not need to calculate or think. And this is a beautiful thing. We do not need to calculate because what we are doing reflects exactly who we are underneath. There are no regrets, all our actions and words are authentic and we loosen up from the outside in and at the same time, the inside out.

> Like all things in this book, spontaneous action is a process that is part of one's daily practice. Spontaneity happens a little bit at a time and it comes when we are wide-open. Sometimes we don't even notice the small changes arising within us. We forgot about the right turn that came without thought, or the sudden reach for eggs instead of oatmeal. This isn't unconscious. We didn't forget and we weren't lost in thought or tired. No, instead we were entirely present, vibrant, and alive. The course of action came out of nowhere. It came from being as opposed to doing and it stemmed, ultimately, from nothing.[62] It is entirely non-linear and it springs out of the now.

These are very small examples, but they are part of the process, leaping out of the mundane as well as the adventurous moments. Is there even a difference? Everything, every moment, every second, is all part of the process. Trusting in spontaneous action not only enriches life, it also increases our intuition, our self-confidence, and our creative abilities. Life is creation. We are creating all the time. Dress, driving style, and gait are all small creative moves we make each and every day. When we plan too much and think too much about outcomes, we dilute much of this creative process. We can still have the pen, but grab a ruler and our canvas is covered in too many straight lines. If we follow the status quo, as followers, our life manifests as such. But we can break out of this by going into the moment and allowing spontaneous action to unfold. Our only framework, our only filter, is our practice. We are mindful, aware, completely in the now, and we live in a way that reflects this with right action, impeccable speech, and clear intentions. We are responsible, we are aspiring Beacons emitting a positive light for others around us to see and feel. But we are also free to be who or what we truly are. When we place faith in what bubbles up, our intuition takes over. We melt into the background and thus we become natural and more fluid. We know that we are becoming less wave-like, and more the sea itself.

> What is more empowering than being able to trust in the natural spring that lies within you?

Spontaneity is wild and outside the confines of what we deem logical or premeditative. These characteristics remain, but when they spring out of our practice, out of the groundless ground within the present in which we are setting down our roots, there is an inherent compassion that coincides with it. I like to think of Bodhidharma's spontaneous answer to Emperor Wu's question, famous in Zen lore, concerning whether or not he had gained merit for funding the construction of monasteries in 5th century China. "No merit," replied Bodhidharma. Out of the vastness, the emptiness at the core of spontaneity, there is no merit – kindness and wildness jut out of the given moment through you.

Surrender

"If you surrender completely to the moments as they pass, you live more richly those moments."

- Anne Morrow Lindbergh

"Better indeed is knowledge than mechanical practice. Better than knowledge is meditation. But better still is surrender of attachment to results, because there follows immediate peace."

- Bhagavad Gita

To know the Self means to be in touch with our inner realms, to be able to reach down, take root and remain calm and clear under any circumstance that might pull us awry. When we have reached a level of dissatisfaction with our own life situation, or when we have come to realize the shallow nature of conditioned existence, in order to change out the old, to deepen, we must be willing to surrender to the greater movements of life and our inner realms, entering into the unknown nature of the present. When we surrender, we become one with who we really are – the witness behind the thoughts. It is what comes forward from the depths – the shadows lurking in the background of our minds – that we must be willing to surrender ourselves to repeatedly. In surrendering, we humbly make the space necessary for unfettered reality to flow through us wholeheartedly and carry us downriver.[63]

> Surrender means letting go of who we thought we were, and being ok with not knowing who or what we are and why we came to be this way.[64] In making space in our lives, we wipe out ideas of what makes us upset, what fills us with joy, what we like, what we dislike, what makes us comfortable and what makes us uncomfortable.

I remember catching a glimpse of an unsettling shadow lurking in my driveway as I walked home at dusk one evening. A warm Santa Ana breeze was blowing down from the mountains, stirring up fallen leaves that crunched with the gravel under my feet. The shape was dark and grainy. It seemed as if it had been thrust out of the opaque twilight sky, and that it was held together by the bark of oak trees that dotted the hillside. There was something deep within me that resonated with the formless shape before me and yet I wanted nothing to do with it. I wanted to run. My entire body was reverberating and I began to sweat. It was uncomfortable to be with this figure, gut-wrenchingly uncomfortable – a feeling that made me squirm and wriggle like a fly caught in a spider's snare. Breathing slowly, allowing the billowing wind and the coming night to swallow me, the shadow and I stood together. I wanted to move, I wanted to get away, and I wanted to break the tension. It would have been so easy. All I had to do was blink and the moment would have shattered, but these options were reactionary and shallow, not sufficient responses for the entity that had entered my zone of awareness. I needed a creative move, so I let go and surrendered myself completely with a deep exhalation and a wide-open demeanor. In surrendering, I went towards the shadow and melted into it. Wooooooosh! The bottom dropped out, the breeze blew and I could feel a large smile crease both our faces.[65] There was a sense of vastness and depth that islands, when viewed from the top of coastal mountains, often give to a panoramic view of the ocean. I was relaxed and yet alert, melting and unpeeling myself into the ground on which I stood.

The shadowy figure was none other than myself, a reflection of the things I had long kept at bay. I could see the phantoms: the crying abandoned little boy, the discomfort, the drinking, the insanity, the masks, the clown, the fear, and the night. The conglomeration of my inner darkness – what I suppressed and what I was uncomfortable wading into – sucked me in and, instead of running away, I saw it as an interesting opportunity for me to shift into a new experience and expand. I had never felt so drained and so light at the same time – a sensation that stemmed from a kind of leap into an apparent black hole.

Later that night I left my home and walked into the hills to sit with the Santa Ana winds, the moon, and my shadow. We laughed together and thought of the mountain lions hungrily looking down on us from the trees – this only made us laugh harder. The shadow visits me from time to time. He comes to receive his gifts, to know that I am here and awake, to know that I do not shun him. I let him come and I accept him with open arms. He is a beautiful boy and I am fortunate to have him sit closer and closer.[66] Though I cannot greet him directly each time, eventually I am pulled in: He comes to pull me down, to rub my face in the soulful dirt of *this* life, to push my practice beyond my borders, and to let me know that when I fall, I am still human. All he requires is my presence and all he asks is that I remain open in the midst of the good and the bad: While I move through the mud of life and while I bask in the warm light of spiritual experience, he teaches me to surrender myself and to treat the myriad possibilities as one. I see now that my shadow, what I run from, is the key to my practice – what I must move towards.

Things become more interesting when we surrender our old notions and habits. Something against which we may have been completely guarded may be the key to a deeper insight, a deeper relationship with ourselves, if we are able to surrender our old beliefs and be open to not knowing what will happen. There is a deliciousness that would otherwise be missing if we did not surrender – we would remain small and guarded, sitting in our metaphorical castles, never knowing what might lay beyond the fog: mountains and trails, the sun, the sky, and the shifting breeze.

> "Love yourself and be awake – today, tomorrow, always. First establish yourself in the way, then teach others, and so defeat sorrow. To straighten the crooked you must first do a harder thing – straighten yourself. You are the only master. Who else? Subdue yourself, and discover your master."
>
> - Buddha

Surrender does not mean to give up or to lie down and wither. Rather, surrender means having the courage to release ourselves to the flow of life. Within total surrender lie natural treasures such as wisdom, strength, and equanimity. The real hero surrenders to the flow because she sees the nature of life. He sees the inherent goodness in the universe and he has faith that life will come to him more fully through letting go of ego, control, and expectation. What seems more difficult? What do most people do? Most people do not face their demons, neurotic behaviors, or conditioned reactions. Many, including myself, smother them with nodding agreement, alcohol, television, food or whatever other recreational habits one can employ to keep shadows at bay. Many people lead an unconscious life. Sometimes we do anything to mask what we are feeling or experiencing, whether we are conscious of it or not. But, if we wish to go beyond this, then what's done is done. Now, we are becoming more conscious, there are no exceptions. An exterior based solution, no matter the activity or the level of righteousness, is out of the inner realms.

Internal strength – spiritual strength – does not come from

physical attributes or chameleon abilities. It does not come from our willingness to fight everything and to defend ourselves from a constant barrage of internal and external twists, turns, and challenges. The better we are at closing ourselves off, the more work must be done to reverse this characteristic, the more we need to turn things around. Those who run fastest to the bottle, conflict, the gym, the store, or the computer in times of trouble are the least in touch with their inner realms. Many people follow such paths in life as a way to cope. Be aware of this reaction in your own mind. Are there any similarities or parallels in your life? Do you happen to go out to things when maybe you should be looking in? If so, please, don't feel bad, just watch and acknowledge. I'm glad you had the willingness to see and to recognize. Be happy now that you have the opportunity to step into wholeness.

An unconscious man or woman will do everything to stop the flow. He will resist, and what he resists will persist or manifest in further negativity and conflict that will inevitably sprout up within other areas of his life. She will criticize, he will fight, he will thrash, and she will squirm. You or I may be materially successful at some point, but when we come to see where true power lies (within surrender) we will see that we have created a sham, a dream based in the exterior that does not mirror our inner Self. It feels shallow. This is where the beauty in Buddhism lies: we learn to test our level of inner alignment for ourselves moment-to-moment.

When we cannot surrender, most of our lives reflect resistance rather than going with what comes. This was how it was for me, and if you look in, it might be this way for you, too. The crux of life – flowing with it, dancing with it – passes and we do not come to know our true Self. We still thirst for more, we desire more. More desire and more gratification of that desire stretch out before us. Continuing the same trends, no matter how we tweak or manipulate them, will not change anything. It is the same fundamental cycle being repeated again and again in a different guise. We can stop the cycle and we can step off the treadmill when we let go of who we think we are. Going beyond our small world and expanding ourselves to encompass more and more of what surrounds us is how we begin to break our perpetual cycles of desire. The most powerful method is through the humble action of surrendering.

One who intimately dives into surrender will be open and receptive to what comes his way. He will know his demons, he will see them lurking and he will not run. He will consciously face them through practicing awareness and mindfulness. He will trust his instincts and he will live in joy through the understanding of the miracle of life. In surrendering to our demons – what we run from – and recognizing them fully, you have successfully broken any attachment to them. Now when they come and dance around you, you watch them calmly and they have nothing to do but fade. Everything becomes clearer when you can surrender to what you run from. So much is freed within, allowing fresh scents and feelings, allowing growth, to come in. Surrender turns darkness to light.

Throughout the day, surrendering to what comes up, whether it is a powerful emotion or a looming dilemma, can make all the difference. By just placing our awareness on what comes up within, we can completely defeat a contentious moment and turn it into light. It is fodder, fuel for us to throw onto our growing flames of daily mindfulness and burning awareness.

When we have the ability to surrender everything, to relinquish control of our image, our ego, and the life we have painstakingly built, then we become free and we begin to flow. As Buddha said,

> "It is better to conquer yourself than to win a thousand battles. Then the victory is yours. It cannot be taken from you, not by angels or by demons, heaven or hell."

Surrender is essential. Buddha comes to the same life-changing conclusion about the meaning of life: know and rule yourself through surrender. To do so means gaining everything the world has to offer, gaining the meaning of living – pure being. Flowing with the river of life is crucial. It is a natural way to be in this world. Stop fighting life right now! When we can accept what is, at this moment, then we can begin to go deeper. We can erase the false images we have created and with which we have surrounded ourselves.

There is great inner strength and a sense of intimacy that comes with surrender. It seems so counterintuitive to our rational, defensive minds – always seeking a tangible success or logical explanation for what is occurring outside, in, and around us. When I could release myself from the snares, when I could let go of the linear narrative, then life seemed to open up in a way I had not experienced before. There is an intimacy that began to show itself to me only when I was able to surrender to past abuses, my likes and my dislikes, and what I deemed comfortable or uncomfortable. Taking down the bricks of my internal walls, letting in the breeze, felt refreshing and natural. You may experience something like this too. Surrender and let go a little more.

Letting Go

The Radiant Buddha said:
Regard this fleeting world
Like stars fading and vanishing at dawn,
Like bubbles on a fast moving stream,
Like morning dewdrops evaporating on blades of grass,
Like a candle flickering in a strong wind,
Echoes, mirages, and phantoms, hallucinations,
And like a dream.

> \- The Eight Similes of Illusion,
> Prajna Paramita Sutra

"He who binds to himself a joy
Does the winged life destroy;
But he who kisses the joy as it flies
Lives in eternity's sunrise"

> \- William Blake

Taking the first steps toward an open and free mind, we must be willing to recognize and let go of the seething attachments in our lives – something that is ingrained in our practice and something I still work with today. Attachments come in many forms. They can be a relationship dynamic, a lifestyle, or hidden within a multiplicity of codependent family, friendly, or romantic partnerships. Walking the path means seeing our attachments as they are: habitual and sometimes neurotic behavioral patterns through which we define our happiness and our sense of security. Recognition of our attachments through the lens of truth and reality is crucial. It is a significant step. Once we recognize such behaviors and see them as they are, we will have no choice but to cut them with our metaphorical sword of mindfulness over time. To continue these patterns, knowing what we know, would only lead to guilt and a false sense of happiness. It is through "attention, attention, attention" that we are able to cut these ingrained patterns.

How many of us turn to externalities or even fabricated moods to become somebody else – to dull the pain of a long workday, or to help us in forgetting some problem? Using alcohol or any other substance is an escape from reality, from ourselves, and what we are feeling internally. Such actions deaden us. If we drink to the point of getting intoxicated, then we are choosing to remove ourselves from the moment, remaining mired in the clutches of our small minds. Drinking is just one example. What about impulsively reaching for food, the remote, a cigarette, a smart phone, or a soda? It's not the action we are looking at, it's the impulse, the need to grasp for these things to comfort ourselves. In doing so, we are not embodying our wholeness. We are denying it. We are running from our Selves and we are running away from the open, spontaneous nature of life. We are escaping from our past while not being able to handle what is happening in the present. We are trying to 'let go' artificially, and this short-term solution does nothing. In fact, it just leads to further unconsciousness and greater separation. To live this way, to rely on something outside of our Selves, to adhere to our impulses, is to live life through the narrow delusions of the ego. We remain shrouded within the fog of a created external world, never being able to touch the innate clarity of the Self.

It was a strange thing to witness my impulsive nature when I first began practicing mindfulness. "Oh, I'm hungry," "Oh, I am upset, so I am going to lift weights!" "I'm bored, I want to watch a scary movie" "She said what? F*ck her, she isn't invited." Yes, it was very interesting to see this and to have the patience to sit down with it – my impulses – without being judgmental. I needed a great deal of patience and some humor. It wasn't that I was evil or misguided, I was just unconscious and I was now becoming aware of the difference between witnessing and self-centeredness. The move that shattered everything, that blew down the walls of my mind, was letting go. "I need to look up Internet videos," transformed into an alert silence. There was a reality in this moment and it was the sun coming through the half-open curtain. It wasn't so much the silence as the experience of suddenly not having a rope around my body or a small weight on my chest. I was experiencing a moment of spaciousness and freedom that no man or woman could give or take from me. There was something inside, below my thoughts, which pushed me to become aware. The action I undertook, that I continue to undertake, is to let go and turn my awareness inwards when the mind begins to churn. Following a rope into my mind, I often found a discomfort or a denial at the core of the streaming impulse. It was time to begin snipping them one by one.

It is very important that we remain mindful that there is nothing wrong or right with us. Our inner voice, our intuitive, connected Self, is speaking up because it sees where we are going and it is trying to stop us from moving permanently into a created, shallow reality. It cries out from time to time, "Wake up! Put that thing down, go outside, be here, see through it all, and let go!" We – I – you are very fortunate that our inner wisdom is always present and accessible. We have the opportunity to break the cycle and to find true happiness and deeper understanding. Anyone is capable of reaching down and seeing *right through*.[67] There is nothing special about consciously letting go until you experience it. And then it just becomes part of life.

> This is the path. You are the path. Don't allow your small, egoic mind to sidetrack you. Witness, be mindful of your thoughts. Don't allow your ego to question what you are doing without seeing and recognizing what is happening.

Initially letting go can be difficult. To renounce the old behaviors and beliefs that comprised the fabric of who you thought you were and to see the reality of your present situation is painful to a certain degree. To understand things that happened in your past as well as the way you remained unconscious through their unfolding, facing them head on, alone, and without your comforting judgments and opinions, is not particularly easy. But within the darkness there are *simple and yet profound* treasures that immediately begin a transformation of your experience. For instance, the sudden experience of freedom: We are free. We can understand this freedom only when we have completely let go of ourselves as well as the tendencies of the small mind. Through practice and occasional walks into the realm of open space, this becomes apparent. What a wonderful, empowering thing to be aware of though. Underneath the surface, we are a free being. "But what would we do!? Who am I if I am free, if I let go, if I don't have any problems, let alone a prescribed way of defining the world?" asks the mind. There is a clinging, a need to hold onto things, to control, which we can witness when we let go. It was interesting and illuminating to see it in action when I stepped back and watched my thoughts. Who was I? Why was I looking into letting go? What would I be? Would any of my close friends understand? Who do I think I am? It wasn't the questions that were illuminating for me, instead, it was the impulse to ask such questions; questions that were afraid of leaving the small world I inhabited. I often grabbed the question and followed a chord back deep into my mind. I was searching for a core, a wound, or some sort of source from which my questions sprang. It became an internal fishing game played out in meditation. There's one doubt, follow it down into the depths! I didn't find a monster, or a giant blue fin tuna. I found my ego, holding on tight, not wanting to leave and step out from the safety of its fortress. I needed to begin to let go, to become free from the inside out.

Allow the realization of freedom to set in. Feel it in your body. Let it permeate through you and for a little bit, just let go. For these few moments we can feel relaxed, at ease, and in the 'experiencer's' seat.

> In spring, hundreds of flowers; in autumn,
> a harvest moon;
> In summer, a refreshing breeze; in winter,
> Snow will accompany you.
> If useless things do not hang in your mind,
> Any season is a good season for you.
>
> - Mumon's commentary on,
> "Everyday Life Is the Path"

Now, before any anxiety sets in again, which it inevitably will – whether it is today or tomorrow, or a week from now – smile and see through, follow the chord down into your mind. See what you just accomplished with this small realization of the most basic thing in life. The most treasured thing in life. See through everything and stare into the core of freedom.

We can cultivate roots that stretch down through our bodies and into the earth. This is good. Letting go and appreciating the ground on which we walk, each moment brings out a kind of reverence for what is. Breathe in the air that sustains us. We let go and touch what lies around us and within us – the inner infinite and the outer infinite – free from the constraints of thoughts or opinions. For we are emptiness, and the river of life flows through our open and accepting nature. We are nothing in the face of the cosmos, and the ego we have created is nothing in the face of our infinite subconscious. And by lightly grasping this concept we will see that we are intricately a part of everything and thus a small piece of the whole. This is something we can all experience deeply at any moment.

Inner truth often feels as if it is deep, profound wisdom that occasionally walks hand-in-hand with ridiculous humor. We are nothing, and in being nothing we are everything. Ahhh relax: Don't ponder this truth. Just let it seep in by letting go of everything.

I am nothing, but I am also everything.

Don't know who you are. Don't know what you are going to do tonight, or when you are going to go for a jog. Just let go and see through everything. Understand that you are linked into the web of the universe. Allow space, let go of who you thought you were or why you should respond in a certain way, and things will magically manifest. Now you are tuned in and you are ready to dig for gold, for everything.

Equanimity

"If you let yourself be blown to and fro, you lose touch with your root. If you let restlessness move you, you lose touch with who you are."

> – Tao Te Ching

"Why do you feel elated when praised and dejected when criticized? It's because you don't accept the way things truly are. You're controlled by your hallucinating mind, which is totally divorced from reality. Your up and down emotions are like clouds in the sky; beyond them, the real, basic human nature is clear and pure."

> – Lama Yeshe

Learning and practicing to live in a way that is removed from the highs and lows of life is learning to live life on the Middle Path. When praise comes, it comes. When criticism comes, it comes. Life comes and goes, rises and falls, and enters the foreground of our experience throughout our fluctuating lives. Witnessing these cycles emanating from the universe, the world, and this moment, and remaining unattached to them, is the path. We understand impermanence, we have a deep perspective, and we are part of the interconnected web that surrounds us. From these understandings and feelings spring equanimity.

There is no need to go up and down with what appears within the mind. This does not mean letting go of joy and anger, no, it means feeling them fully as they come, and through this, allowing them to move past and then fade naturally. Living this way empowers us. Equanimity is the embodiment of deep roots in the earth, this body, and this life. We are stable in the face of all comings and goings. The natural movement of the world manifests and transforms, and we are but a mirror, like a pond reflecting the moon.

> Like space, equanimity is an internal medium through which all things move. Open and alive, grounded, one who embodies equanimity embodies all things and allows them to pass through unencumbered.

No matter the storm, no matter the stress, no matter the ecstasy, someone who has mastered equanimity remains even and grounded. Every time we turn the light of our consciousness inward, every time we witness the mind through mindful attention and present-moment awareness, we strengthen our roots in the earth. Like the tree, our roots not only bring stability and connection, they bring us nutrients in the form of wisdom and understanding. Roots ground us into what *is* – the Self, and the infinite it is a part of each and every moment. As we move from location to location, our roots come with us, for they are within us. We remain centered, wherever we are.

When you have come to reach down to your inner Self, life changes, your form changes, but the inner core you are grounded in remains vast. The witness is born. We watch things come and go as the tree watches the shades of day. We feel, we witness, and through this, we are nourished. There is a basic, unjustified joy that comes from just watching the unfolding of life and flowing with what comes. Contentment ensues. Wisdom ripens. We stabilize in the here and now. If we can plant the seed of mindfulness and if we practice reaching into our core, what moves, moves. The tree, however, remains unmoving, nourished by the natural flow: the rain, the sun, and all the fluctuations in-between.

The Zen story below illustrates the balance of a true redwood, Zen Master Hakuin:

> The Zen Master Hakuin (1686-1769) travelled extensively to learn from other masters. When he was 32 years old, he returned to the Shoin-ji, the temple in his home town of Hara, in present-day Shizuoka Prefecture. Here he devoted himself to teaching a growing number of disciples. Hakuin was praised by his neighbors as a teacher living an exemplary life.

A beautiful Japanese girl whose parents owned a food store lived near him. One day without warning, her parents discovered that she was pregnant.

This made her parents angry. The girl would not confess who the man was, but after much harassment, she named Hakuin as the father.

In great anger the parents went to the Zen Master and scolded him in front of all his students. All Hakuin would say was "Is that so?"

After the baby boy was born, it was entrusted to Hakuin's care. By this time he had lost his reputation. His disciples had left him. However Hakuin was not disturbed, and enjoyed taking care of the little boy. He obtained milk and other essentials the boy needed from his neighbors.

A year later, the girl-mother couldn't stand it any longer. She confessed the truth to her parents— that the real father of the boy was not Hakuin but a young man working in the local fish market. The father and mother of the girl went to Hakuin at once. They asked his forgiveness and apologized profusely to get the boy back.

Although Hakuin loved the child as his own, he was willing. In giving up the boy, all he said was: "Is that so?"

> \- Paul Reps, *Zen Flesh, Zen Bones* (1957)

"Is that so?" Hakuin's story reveals a luscious quality in life that comes with sitting patiently amid change. Staying rooted into being (having faith in ourselves as Lin-chi would say), Hakuin treated change, which sprang out of nowhere, as a gracious host would treat a humble guest. I often look to this story to remind myself how unpredictable and bizarre life can be and how a true Zen master deals with change. But at the same time, Hakuin's equanimity teaches me to turn around my thoughts and notions and see how 'un-bizarre' any event is in the face of endless change. Everything is part of the myriad possibilities. Whether we are dealt a blow, a newborn baby, a fall crimson leaf, or drops of rain, all these externalities reverberating around us continue to do so. The question is: how much do we allow what is happening outside ourselves to sweep us off our feet? How often do we allow the natural turn of the world and the change that comes with it to bring us down or shoot us up into the clouds? Resting in our bodies and watching our own minds meditatively, we can experience a calm serenity not unlike the master's above.

Meditation helped me gain more balance in my life. As we meditate, we consciously nourish our roots – the essential aspect of equanimity – by giving them the space and conscious energy to reach down into the moist earth and fertile subconscious. There is a vastness within we can touch each day through simply watching ourselves as we move through busy days, slow days, hectic days, languid days, and competitive days. There is something below all this change and labeling that remains constant – an equanimity that is in each and every one of us, lying patiently and fully aware. All we have to do is cut through our thoughts and turn the excessive nature of our outward-looking mind back in on itself to uncover it.

For me, equanimity came slowly. Months passed and still, storm after storm blew me off course. Compliments and criticisms pushed me about. But what I didn't realize was the slow, creeping effect meditation was having on my life. My reactions began to change. I noticed that something that would have driven me mad just a few weeks before had become funny to me. I would laugh at the strivings of my mind and see how unnecessary they were. I had everything I needed to nourish me right here, in this moment and in this mind. And within that switch came the vastness of being ok with things that hadn't been ok for me before. There wasn't any denial or repression, just a mental tweak that allowed the moment to be exactly as it was. Letting things be, then, allowed me to open up and greet the moment with more compassion and reverence.

Roots come, but they grow slowly. When we plant a corn seed, we don't immediately harvest corn or put it in the microwave to make popcorn the next day. Plant equanimity and balance through consciousness. It takes time and patience. It takes conscious watering to reap the reward. I watered it daily through meditation and mindfulness – not perfectly, but to the best of my beginner's abilities. With time, balance showed itself. The occasional argument would rear its head "Rarrrrrrr," and I watched. I listened to what was being said and I remained concentrated on the individual or the situation. I listened without defensiveness. The insults came and they went and I listened, rooted into my core. My roots felt strong and I was in touch. But these examples shift. The question to ask here is, "What will we do when life tests us, when the insult flies or the pain comes into our 'important' lives?" We do not always pass these tests. But what is certain is that we can learn and with each test, through practice, we can stand up again, set our feet, and grow our roots deeper into the ground.

"If you fall on the ground, stand up by the ground."
– Zen Master Dogen

The Zen Master's words have deep significance: get up off the same ground you find yourself on. The ground is simply life, the here and now, the experiences that push and pull us. For it is within these very moments, the ones that test us and shake us to our core, the ones we fail to understand, that present us with the opportunities for the most profound type of growth.[68] When we become intimate with the ground we have fallen upon, with the mud, we are able to go beyond who we thought we were. It is not about finding a crutch through escaping to some activity or reaction: no, equanimity comes when we are able to put our own two hands in the mud and push ourselves up from the very thing that is driving us into delusion. Nagging parents, volatile lovers, low bank account figures, these are the moments where we will grow the most if we are able to jump into, "Is that so?" It is difficult, I cannot stress that enough, but it is also very possible for all of us. Are we open to this?

It can be difficult to rest in non-judgment. The cultivation of equanimity requires a humbleness that is founded in one's ability to watch the ego and, particularly, its need to label things and to react. When we can step away from our impulses, when we can see the world from the context of vastness, and especially during times of adversity, equanimity creeps forth.

I ask now, what is better? Losing it, having the need to fight back? Proving our stance to feel a false sense of pure ego pride, or knowing one's Self? Being able to listen fully and understand where the other is coming from, being able to speak our truth calmly and completely, speaking and acting impeccably – not so much for the other, but for our Self, is the Way.

Equanimity does not mean sitting balanced between the two extremes of reaction and non-reaction – aggressiveness, passive aggressiveness, and self-righteousness. No, it means to go beyond these states to something higher – to transcend the poles. This transcendence comes from what we gain and what we shed in our search for the Self. When our Self emerges, balance emerges. It is completely natural. Praise, blame, and everything in-between are all waves crashing around in the exterior world – we find that all ups and downs reside within the one.[69] When we are rooted, the waves appear just as waves. We are below them in the stillness of the ocean, watching them crash about. And, sometimes, when we are clear and present, we see those we know and even ourselves, riding and wiping out.

Watch yourself. Go to the deep. Sink your roots into the Self and into the now.

> "Be not angry that you cannot make others as you wish them to be, since you cannot make yourself as you wish to be."
> - Thomas à Kempis, *Imitation of Christ*, c.142

Equanimity enhances our intuition and we begin to trust it more and more. We enter a new place and we are better able to feel it because we know our Selves. The images of the movie continue to change, but the screen, our balanced Self, remains the same. To be balanced is to transcend existence truly. By just being, we are in the present moment and life flows as it does.

Presence

"You can't seem to stop your mind from racing around everywhere and seeking something. That's why the ancestors said, 'Hopeless fellows using their heads to look for their heads!' You must right now turn your light around and shine it on yourselves, not go seeking somewhere else. Then you will understand that in body and mind you are no different from the Ancestors and Buddhas, and that there is nothing to do. Do that and you may speak of 'getting the Dharma.' "

- Zen Master Lin-chi

Presence can be described as pure being. To be means to be aware of what is right here, right now, both inside and out. It requires no grasping, no thought, no visualization, just placement of your unwavering attention in the here and now. At first this can be difficult because it involves a huge amount of mindful concentration. Some of us have been out of touch for quite some time.

Oftentimes we space out to save energy.
We detach in order to protect ourselves.
We build fortresses and walls to hide behind.
We stroll down deadening avenues for comfort.
We live behind masks and created mental projections –
dampening our connection and losing touch with reality.

Being *alert* in the here and now requires genuine being – something we may do on and off throughout the day, if ever. Our small minds do not like being because to be present means to have no use for the planning mind and the streaming narrative of thoughts in our heads. To be present means we are natural, we are here. When something arises, we give it our full attention and we respond from a place far deeper than the mind. The ego does not want natural, it wants to be in control – to plan, to judge, to criticize, to predict, and to inhabit a subjective mental idea of reality.

Whether we recognize presence in ourselves or in those around us, it is easy to notice when someone is not 'here.' We can notice when we are not paying attention, when we are thinking about what we will say next or fantasizing about being somewhere else. There are people who are very good at not being present while appearing to be completely involved in what is happening around them, but with practice, it is easy to see through those masks, too, within ourselves and others. We may be one of these people, just going through the motions. We may be thinking about something else or worrying about how we look, or thinking about when someone is going to call us to tell us something important. I experienced this most of the time myself, and, from my experience, I think there are others who might be able to relate.

> Recognition and acceptance of our past behaviors – the ways we take ourselves out of the now – and bringing this recognition into our present experience is all that is asked. Authentic pure being and pure presence are the goals, and witnessing when we are drifting off into our thoughts is the first step.

The ego takes us out of the now as a way to empower itself and, simultaneously, as a way to use more vital energy. Every time we remove ourselves from the present by thinking or fantasizing, we are not fully alive and we are using our energy to maintain this state of going through the motions. Just as a computer employs a screensaver to save power, so too does the mind. Mental fantasies of lying on a beach or imagining a beautiful lover are simply mental 'mind savers.' Each time we do this, the small mind gains more and more strength by claiming more and more of our daily energy. We can stop this by witnessing the 'mind saver' taking place and removing ourselves from it the moment we begin to notice. No matter how long we slip into a daydream state, calmly removing ourselves immediately empowers us and focuses our natural energy back into the present moment.

"When you do something, you should burn yourself completely, like a good bonfire, leaving no trace of yourself"
- Roshi Shunryu Suzuki

Suzuki's words touch on a way of living that is free from mental baggage or restrictions. When we are present, we become enmeshed in what we are consciously undertaking. Rather than leaving behind unfinished business, boredom, doubt, or various shades of resentment, all that remains is open space. Both our egos and the activity we are in are burned within our focused awareness, and all that is left is whatever is happening in the now we find ourselves in – in other words, unencumbered reality.

Being fully present is a different way to go about our busy lives, and I often find the practice of continued awareness tiring. But I also realize how much more alive I am when my presence is burning and I am completely in the moment. Going about my daily business lost in thought – what I had been doing my entire life – felt hazy and almost dream-like. Where was I? What just happened? As I stepped in and out of my practice, it felt as though I was stepping in-between two worlds: one that was small, subjective and entirely in my head, and another that was pure, borderless, and vastly beyond comprehension. There was a connection that reached far deeper into my existence when I was in the latter of these two worlds, and I enjoyed the freedom that came with sitting hand-in-hand with the now.[70]

Begin practicing mindfulness by remaining in the present moment. Focus on the breath, allow feelings to flow through without getting attached, and stay alert as much as possible. Try it for one day. Be the witness of what occurs. Concentrate on your actions without worrying about the fruit they bear or drifting out of the now through judgmental thoughts.

Just be in what you are doing, concentrating fully on what is taking place right here, right now. There is nothing else. See what happens to you. If you truly commit for one day, you will most likely be exhausted. But, you will experience what it is like to be truly *here*, outside the confines of the ego. With time, as you continue to open up the innateness within, your presence will become more natural and your awareness will grow. Opening up and entering into the vastness of the now is a joyful and interesting experience. Bringing our attention back to the now, the 'thusness' of life is there to greet us: "Oh, there it is!"

Our energy will increase dramatically if we continue, because we are cultivating authenticity. Authentic being, or presence, is a different energy. It is focused, clear, vibrant, and it is a completely natural product. It comes from within, and it is always there, ready to be tapped into. But it has been replaced by dream energy. We are used to shutting down throughout the day, allowing the small mind and the "mind saver" to come in and run the ship, and this has permeated our daily dealings. Rather than truly listening, we think. Rather than being, we space out. Rather than witnessing, we watch the television. The list goes on.

When you sincerely begin your practice,

Within the present realize the true Self.
Past is in the present, future is in the present.

Blow down the walls of conceptualization, of worry, fear, and subjective perception. These barriers are of our own making. See through them and consciously remove them. This is all possible through placing ourselves in the right here, right now. Being present is being humble and powerful. One who is present, who embodies presence, is free.

Impermanence

"You live in illusion and the appearance of things. There is a reality. You are that reality, but you don't know it. If you wake up to that reality, you will know that you are nothing, and being nothing, you are everything. That is all."
                                        - Kalu Rinpoche

"Long live impermanence!"
                                        - Thich Nhat Hanh

"Everything flows and nothing abides,
Everything gives way and nothing stays fixed"
                                        - Heraclitus

Impermanence is simply another name for reality. Things change, and when it comes to our youth, our friendships, our homes, our families, our pets, anything we have become attached to, watching them go can be excruciatingly painful. And yet, we know that our attachments, like us, will disappear, transform, and cease to exist in this world of ever-shifting forms.[71]

> The first step in contemplating impermanence is to become aware of it and to accept the fact that all things change, and are changing, whether we want them to or not. It is within the acceptance of this evident truth that we move out of ignorance and step into reality. It is also within the contemplation of the impermanent nature of life that we can cultivate a deep appreciation for each moment we inhabit as it is.

Things happen and then, as soon as they arrive, they disappear.[72] What seemed so important yesterday – the test, the interview, the game – passed away and is gone. Like vivid dreams, forms, circumstances, and events rise and then fade into the past. Think about the college final that meant everything. Where is it now? What happened to it? What about the job interview or the big date in ninth grade? Though these events were extremely important in the context of our life situation then, they have become memories. Conversely, when we continue to base our lives on the next event, the next thing, the future, we realize that lasting peace and joy cannot come from this way of living because it has nothing to do with this moment. And when we desperately expect an outcome, we only add to the inevitable sensation of dissapointment. Living in the past, occupying the future, or genuinely believing that something will last forever are at odds with how life functions, and thus, how we function. There is a conflict then between our minds and the world we move through that does not have to exist if we just let go and accept the fundamental truth of impermanence. Natural change teaches us that in the end, no matter how much we strive to control or resist, the vastness reclaims each and every one of us. This is a humbling and beautiful conclusion to rest against and melt into. There is nowhere for the small mind to hide, and thus an infinite space for the moment to manifest freshly.

> To touch our inner core and to do so in the context of seeing the impermanent nature of life, we come to a deeper understanding, one that allows us to remain stable and unwavering, below the movement of unending – rising and falling – waves.

Our emphasis of the external in the contemporary world is a major flaw that negates the true nature of being, of existence. For things manifest and then they are gone. It is a natural process. The next goal or object of our intention comes, and then it too is gone. It is simply gone. When we see this truth, we come to the deep realization of impermanence. "You cannot step into the same river twice," is what keeps life interesting and also, possible. Why fight the very law that gives rise to us? We were thrust from impermanence and we return in a blink of an eye.

Our attachment to form perpetuates a constant cycle of delusion. We watch something come, we attach to it, we grasp it, we impose our will on the outcome, and then we suffer the results, whether what we want occurred or did not occur. We wait in the trough for a moment and then, "Look," we say, "Another wave to ride up!" The next event comes and we repeat. Over and over we do this for our entire lives. We do not see the true nature of life – the ebb and flow of the tides, the natural cycles within the cycles of the world and the universe.[73]

When I looked into the Buddhist notion of impermanence, I began to question my rigid opinions on what I believed to be right or wrong. My grandmother's passing, the leafless oak in winter, quitting my job, and the slow decline of an old friendship, were all painful events that had unfolded throughout my life situation. They were standard, universal human events which course through each person's experience in some form or another. What was wrong with these events in my life then? The more I examined the 'darker,' 'negative' episodes in my life, the more I found that the events themselves were not bad; they were part of a much larger picture, and in most cases, they led to a deeper understanding of the world. These moments, grounded in impermanence, were interconnected with moments of relief, new friendships, love, growth, wisdom, and space. All were part of the same universal fabric.

The disconnection between my understanding of impermanence and my reaction to the pain of moving through a seemingly dicey transitional period in my life was what I delved into most. Why was I so small? Why was it hard for me to take in the entire scene? Why did I have to react and resist the natural flow? I felt separate and encased, and the only way to move out of my shell was to begin accepting the impermanence of everything: my thoughts, the dog, the tree, a rusty can, my physique, the actress' beauty. They were all wonderful, and the prospect of their passing made them each that much more wonderful. Looking into impermanence was yet another way to create a bond with life that ran much deeper than what I had previously experienced. I was not the center of the universe, and I, whatever I was, needed to be here to reap the miraculous moment. It seems a little lofty, appreciating everything and seeing through the core of emptiness within all objects and beings, but it is reality and reality, is a gift. Why pretend it is any other way?

Yes, living without understanding or seeing impermanence is ok. It is still an experience in the world in and of itself. We will all realize impermanence the day we die. In the meantime, we expand our mental capacity and we are able to make a living and inhabit our egos. This is good in the context of survival. But did we live fully? Did we gain deeper peace, happiness, joy, or true love? Did we create harmony, did we become a compassionate person, did we strive to touch the lives of others? And, most importantly, did we come to know our true inner Self? We can strive and fight and be successful, but in the end, we will become a pair of dates resting on a slab of stone. And eventually we will be nutrients for the plants poking out of the soil above us! This is the reality, the binding fate that connects all of us to the interconnected web of life. You too will fade and those you love, the things you cherish, will do the same. There is nothing bad or wrong with this. Of course, losing someone hurts. We miss him or her, but what happened was not bad. Death, the end of a career, recycling the body, is not bad. Without impermanence there could be no birth, no transformation, no change, and ultimately, no life.

> Impermanence, like the tide, cleanses the present moment. Accepting impermanence as a natural part of life is the key step.

The view of reality through the lens of impermanence will change your life for the better because it allows you to see the cycles as they are. Whether it is a passing of a loved one or a deep emotional loss, our attachment to and judgment of what is and our conceptualization of what happens distorts truth. What happened simply happened. We will greatly appreciate the miracle of life and our level of inner peace will grow if we can accept impermanence. And when we accept, we can begin to play with the notion too, for nothing is set in stone, nothing is known. Science has postulated that there is a set amount of energy in this universe. Energy cannot be created or destroyed, just changed. Things manifest and then they change, and death is part of this ongoing recycling process. As a seed germinates into a flower and the flower decomposes into nutrients for soil, life moves and flows in this way.

Through turning in, impermanence becomes more evident and accepted. When the ego is removed, impermanence just is, like the sky or a towering mountain. This feeling comes from tapping into a natural truth, one that is understood only through looking deeply at the nature of life. Wisdom is what we get to take with us to enrich our lives. It is the gift of impermanence. And to live with this newly found wisdom is to live life that much more fully. We move with ease, and yet, with a greater purpose, we know our place in the vastness of the background. Each moment we are not here is a wasted moment. Our time is precious.

In making space for impermanence, I am not saying that we should let go of life. I am not being pessimistic. On the contrary, I am asking you to examine the nature of life without the interference of judgment. When we understand the perpetual cycles of form, we come to the deeper truth of impermanence. And when we see the true nature of form, our suffering will decrease, for we will see things as they are and we will be given an opportunity to become free of the small mind. We will not be attached to the outcome. We will not resist what occurs. We see something, we watch, we act accordingly, in a way reflecting the phrase, "Being in this world, but not of it," and then we let go of an outcome completely, shifting into the now.

Losing our tight grip on outcomes will be the best thing that ever happened to us because we will start living a realized, conscious life. When we live in a state of Y, for example and all we can focus on is the desired X. Then what happens to the space in between? What happens to time, our life experience? And then what happens when the desired X becomes a Z? "Wasted time, and on top of all of it, I get a Z! This is horrible!" We are expecting and not experiencing: life is passing us by and we watch it pass like a bird in a cage.

> Change, no matter what kind, in the grand scheme of things, is something that should be cherished. Life needs

change to continue and thrive. Galaxies need supernovas, black holes, and budding stars. Something ceases and then something rises out of nowhere.

We will be more involved in what we do if we stare through the lens of impermanence. Seeing life as it is adds a dimension of appreciation – a reverence for the infinite range of possibilities we pass through in each moment. We can understand: "That will be gone soon so I must appreciate it. I will be gone soon, so I must be here right now, fully present, and aware of all that is taking place." Having this attitude enriches life. It does not keep us chained to a cave wall: on the contrary, it is our walking stick that aids us in our quest out of the cave in which we have been mulling about.[74]

Balance, equanimity, and truth all lay at the center of the realization of impermanence. There is no need to swing between highs and lows. Just being is all that matters. Compliments come and go. Criticisms come and go. There is no need to get attached to these things, for they are just fleeting manifestations. Give them your full attention and let them go. You already know the nature of life, and in time, you will know the truth at your core, the truth of Self. The truth is already in you and it must come out through your own realization of impermanence.

Life moves. It is fluid and it is complex beyond conceptualization, beyond understanding. Try to control the river and it will keep us wrapped in delusion. We will think that we are in control, but in the end, we are just running, unable to see the small whirlpool life has placed us in – a little eddy within the context of the great river. Realize this truth, let go, and jump into the river of life with no strings attached.

> Stagnation stinks, literally. Keep it fresh, let things pass, and be open to diving into new arenas.

Buddha compared each human's life to that of a lightning bolt. He saw each life as a brilliant flash that faded into the storm cloud as soon as it appeared. The Buddha's profound wisdom simply points to reality exactly as it is. In the context of the universe, our life is a flash in the cosmic show, melting back into the cloud that bore it. This is not pessimism. It is reality. Why not accept this? Why not incorporate this view into our daily lives so we can appreciate each moment without denying what is? What happens next isn't logically clear, for it is beyond the scope of the intellectual mind. All we know is that energy, what we are made of, transforms. Where? Maybe you will discover this on your path... But for now, focus on the life that is here. What is known right now? Our bolt of lightning is lighting up the sky and this is all we need to know: fall headlong into impermanence and embrace it tenderly.

Seeing impermanence allows us to be free of the petty things that constantly consume our time and energy. Having the attitude of "right here, right now," releases us from the chains of the ego. Death in itself can be the greatest teacher of all because it reminds us of our own brief existence. We rarely think about death or the passing of things because we fear the idea of it, but death is natural and there is no denying its necessity for life. Death, change, and transformation are here, and we probably have had some experience with them in our lives: family members, the changing seasons, or a dying thunderhead. When we are able to accept impermanence and release our focus out onto the infinite background, death becomes just a part of the process. Without it, there would be no life and no room for the freshness of change to seep in and cleanse the old. No room for the journey.

Karma

"Whatever we do lays a seed in our deepest consciousness, and one day that seed will grow."

- Sakyong Mipham[75]

"The thought manifests as the word;
The word manifests as the deed;
The deed develops into habit;
And habit hardens into character.
So watch the thought and its ways with care,
And let it spring from love born out of concern for all beings."

- Buddha

Karma is a thought, word, action, or habit that contributes to the cycle of cause and effect within our lives. Yes, even our thoughts contribute to our karma. It is a very simple rule that runs twenty-four hours a day, seven days a week. There is no running from karma. It is the basic law of cause and effect: think a nasty thought, and that nastiness will return to your life at some point and in some unknowable form in the future. With this in mind, it is important to cleanse ourselves of negativity, judgment, and reaction. That doesn't seem so bad does it? Regardless of whether one believes in reincarnation, karma is a tangible part of our daily lives.

Do you ever think about bad days and how they seem to build off something or feed on themselves? For example, you drop your keys, then you drop your phone, then you call yourself a klutz, then you stain your dry-cleaning or receive a parking ticket, then you get upset, then you become negative… There is a strange, noticeable cycle to these "bad days." And yet, oftentimes we just keep plowing through unconsciously, without ever stopping to see what is happening around or within us. We can either become wrapped up in unconsciousness, or we can stop for a few moments to examine ourselves and see how our karma – our presence and our internal dialogue – may be playing a role in what is occurring around us.

When I watched myself and listened to my internal dialogue during stressful times, I noticed how angry and forceful my thoughts were. I was very defensive and reactive to what was happening. I would become closed-off or testy – out of sync and off-balance. It was while I practiced mindfulness that I actually became aware of how I was incurring more of the same nagging events in different areas of my life. Losing myself in one instance morphed into another one down the road. As long as I was out of touch with my thoughts and reactions, my karmic cycle would manifest again and again over time. Through accepting karma and watching my thoughts, I could claim more and more of the moment. Life just happened and there was a spaciousness that surrounded whatever came into the foreground of my mind.

When we finally come to understand karma we see that painful events don't stop. There are still responsibilities and accidents, traffic and cracked windows. Life continues to churn. What changes, however, is our reaction and the ensuing depth of a growing equanimity. The Zen masters said that karma was an illusion grounded in our beliefs of good and bad – duality – thoughts, and our ignorance of oneness. Rather than the shit hitting the fan, through practice we might see that ultimately, within the present, the fan and the shit are one.[76] The question is, you. Where is there a place for shit to stick within an infinite Self?

Rough days are tests for us to work with. Things happen out of nowhere, and we have a choice of how we dance with the moment. How do we stop these cycles and how do we turn the negative moments into positive opportunities? A heated moment arises: do we react over-aggressively at the time? Do we internalize it and bad-mouth the individual later to our friends? Do we act unconsciously – lost in thoughts, emotions, defensiveness, avoidance, etc, or do we act consciously – completely present, attentive to the situation? We can bring about a profound change in our lives through the latter, while the former keeps us spinning on the hamster wheel.

There is an old Zen story about a Master who would call out loudly to himself each morning, "Master?" He would respond, "Yes!" Again he would ask himself, "Are you awake...?" The Master would holler out, "Yes! Yes!" – signaling his complete presence. When we expand this example to the karmic world in which we live, we can view life as an exchange; a relationship between the world and ourselves. The world throws something at us, calling out, "Master? Are you awake?" With a conscious response we return a vibrant, "Yes! Yes!" This is transmuting your karma. This is stepping out of the wheel of unconsciousness. The more conscious we are, the more we remove ourselves from the cycle.

Our Karma is our own. It is not someone else's doing. Blaming or reacting impulsively is weakness, or more accurately, ignorance. When we take hold of our own karma, we take responsibility for everything happening around us. We see it as a reflection of the internal – not in a negative or positive way, not in a judgmental way, but rather in a way that is born of total acceptance and clear vision.

Imagine a stream passing effortlessly past rocks and fallen branches, leaf piles and precipitous falls. When we take responsibility for our karma, we become like the water itself flowing, following the slope that leads toward the sea. Without hesitating or thinking, water passes around the obstacle fluidly in a way that invokes grace, a spontaneous caress. Without stopping to check the depth of the cavern, water passes right through, knowing nothing of darkness or light. When we can flow with life, when we are grounded in a sterling practice of mindfulness, karma is diluted, and for some, it all but disappears.

The Sword Of Mindfulness

"Mindfulness is the aware, balanced acceptance of the present experience. It isn't more complicated than that. It is opening or receiving the present moment, pleasant or unpleasant, just as it is, without either clinging to it or rejecting it."

- Sylvia Boorstein

"Taia is the name of an ancient sword that has no equal under heaven. This famous jeweled sword can freely cut anything, from rigid metal and tempered steel to dense and hardened gems and stones. Under heaven there is nothing that can parry this blade... All men are equipped with this sharp sword Taia, and in each one it is perfectly complete. This means that the famous Sword Taia, which no blade under heaven can parry, is not imparted to other men. Everyone, without exception, is equipped with it, it is inadequate for no one, and it is perfectly entire."

- Takuan

Throughout the day our minds are racing from one thing to the next. Oftentimes we get caught up in these thoughts, and then emotions are produced. Our perception of what is occurring around us becomes distorted by our own projections and beliefs, and before we know it, we are completely lost and out of touch with reality. When we are not mindful of our thoughts, when we are not aware of our surroundings, and when we are not concentrated on the present moment, we fall prey to illusion and, ultimately, disconnection from reality. Our dream is in full swing and the wild flow of life is forced to fit our conceptual prisms and squares. We resist, we judge, and we become attached to our mental projections and fantasies. Our need to defend ourselves in arguments, our need to stand out at a social gathering, our need to impress, to act compulsively, to be someone else, all stem from losing touch with our inner Self. The practice of mindfulness brings us back and restores the essential connectivity to the now.

To quell the mind and the ego we must employ something capable of slicing through mental fabrications and unexamined emotions. And that tool is the sword of mindfulness, of truth, of reality – the Sword of Taia. If you are not firmly anchored in the now, and if you continue to identify with externalities, i.e. anything other than the Self, then the sword will prove most effective for you. Have it at your side at all times and be diligent, be disciplined. Learn to become a peaceful warrior, a Bodhisattva. The title is only there to aid you. Let it ground you into being and inspire you to become a light for yourself and for others who cannot see in the dark – those still dwelling in the cave of conditioned existence.

When I first delved into my spiritual practice, like most novice practitioners, I was able to experience periods of clear vision. These powerful moments of clarity could last hours. During these experiences, everything flowed so well. "Of course," I thought, "This is the Way, this is the path, ahhhh." However, these inner states of understanding would eventually be overwhelmed by the projections in my head. I would become frustrated and agitated with myself. How could an angry driver or a long day suddenly nullify my view of the miracle of life? Why was I so weak? I would then be consumed by doubt – a destructive creation of the mind that is nevertheless *just* a creation of the mind. Despite my understanding of the benefits of mindfulness and also the power of the mind as a hindrance to the path, I would still become a victim of doubt and the internal stirrings of my ego.

To move beyond this, I began to visualize a tool that I could employ against negative thoughts and emotions that distorted my clear sight – something that could slice through the dream and reveal, once again, the inner calm and stillness of my conscious being. The tool was the sword of truth, of reality, and my mantra was, *"Mindfulness, Awareness, Concentration, and Acceptance of what is."* Whenever a tense emotion arose, such as anger, I recognized it, I became still, I breathed, and I cut through it swiftly. What lay before me was awareness. The anger was just a creation of the mind that had absolutely no effect on my inner being. It had no bearing on my life whatsoever, but it struggled to maintain the existence and domination of my small mind. Though the anger would linger, it had lost its roots and thus its power over me. It became a ghost and it dissipated into the nothingness that bore it. Gaining the ability to influence my state of being seemed more powerful than relying on manipulation or defensiveness.

A key component of the sword lies in the final phrase of the mantra, *"Acceptance of what is,"* or recognizing the nature of the mind. Thoughts, emotions, and mental fabrications are all part of the mind. In the quest for inner understanding, we often feel pushed or blown around by these feelings. The intensified highs of clear vision and awareness in contrast to the lows of old, caged mental reactions and habits, can feel overwhelming, even obliterating. We become frustrated with ourselves and we question our resolve in what we are doing. Be patient. These feelings of doubt can be recognized and released when we confront them with the sword.

The feeling of anger is not bad. Anger and all the other emotions are natural phenomena of the mind. There is absolutely nothing wrong with anger, or you, for that matter, for feeling angry. When we label anger as bad or 'negative,' then we set up a dualistic battle inside ourselves of good versus evil. Fighting leads to more fighting. Treat anger with love and space by accepting it and seeing its true nature, its necessary existence. The point is to realize that we are not the emotion, but rather the deep being who is experiencing it. Witnessing creates space, and with more space, where is there a place for an emotion to cling?

Anger and happiness exist side by side and are part of the spiritual path. Without the two, there could be no practice and thus no understanding of equanimity. Anger, fear, and grief are all there to be witnessed and treated with consciousness and the cutting edge of the sword of mindfulness. We can only feel our emotions and allow them to pass through us by seeing their roots springing from our created ego. Just feel their presence and allow them to pass without becoming attached. See them, smile at them, and let all tense emotions drift into the nothingness once more. Negative and positive fall to pieces before the vastness of the deeper Self.

When you begin, the small mind will amaze you at its ability to judge, criticize, run incessantly, sexualize, dramatize, etc. The list is long. Remember that you have just lit a match and that the match must be protected with mindfulness, awareness, concentration, and acceptance of what is. With time, the small ember of consciousness will grow into a sustainable flame. Remain in the present moment and continue to cultivate the flame, but do not be hard on yourself if your match is occasionally extinguished.

> "You can search throughout the entire universe for someone who is more deserving of your love and affection than you are yourself, and that person is not to be found anywhere. You yourself, as much as anybody in the entire universe deserve your love and affection."
>
> - Buddha

Our projections not only affect our moods, but also our interactions with others. My anger or my insecurity can completely distort my relationship with another human whom I perceive as threatening or challenging. In reality, that human is just another being living his or her life. The majority of us live most of our lives like this. We project, we defend, we fight, we mistrust, we assume, judge, and act unconsciously. When we live life unconsciously, we perpetuate cycles of negative energy. These waves ripple out and affect others. The person we judged feels our negative energy and mirrors it back. He or she continues her day projecting and defending. Now imagine this on a global scale: small egocentric waves of unconsciousness bouncing off one another. When we become conscious, when we can see clearly and sanely, we become beings that emanate a vibrant presence – a sheltered inlet for those moving in the turbulence of roiling seas and unceasing dream cycles.

Unconscious individuals see their reflections in those who are conscious and they have two paths: one, to examine themselves, or option two, to react and continue to live out an unconsciously driven reality. Just as a child fears the deep end of the pool and shies away from it, so too does a shallow, unconscious ego avoid the depth it senses within consciousness. However, some might see the light in those who use the sword, and they experience a sudden upwelling of curiosity. They see what a conscious swordsman represents. That is the power of your nascent awakening. Some people will want to change because of you, and every person you touch will have the power to touch others, too. Though you can only work on your Self, it is nice to know what consciousness can bring to the world. When you are present, you are what the Buddha calls a Bodhisattva, a very conscious individual who remains in this world to deepen and to aid others. The magical thing is that you do not have to do anything. Your natural and inherent presence is all that is required of you.

We live in a society that can be shallow and concentrated on getting more or going farther rather than being present. There might be something wrong with this, an inherent flaw that could be as clear as day. We might never be truly happy if we live this way. With this in mind, it is ok to drop the sword every now and again. Pick it up and continue with more resolve and a deeper understanding.

Having the sword and the mantra changed my life because it helped me increase my consciousness. Balance, equanimity, understanding, and even wisdom became more evident in my daily interactions. My vision was clearer and my tendency to judge, to criticize, and to resist the present faded a little. More and more often I could say no when I wanted to say no, and yes when I wanted to say yes. I changed as an individual because I was peeling away the layers and reaching down into my core. As I became more aware of myself and my surroundings, a steady joy bubbled to the surface that came from nowhere. Joy that came for no reason other than the appreciation of being. Little, ordinary things became extraordinary. Life became an amazing experience and I did not want to miss a second of it. It's fun to step out of cloudy delusion for a while – to look around and breath with the sky before falling back into 'good' and 'bad.'

Using the sword and the mantra will change your life, too. There is nothing quite like having the ability to truly be the master and commander of your experience. When you can clear the mental fabrications and see through them, into their inner nature, your being is uncovered. Though it is often only momentary, a moment of being reveals the inherent joy and calm that lie underneath the ego and the concepts, drama, emotions, and fabrications of mind. The fog clears and you see the sky. As your practice continues, you will come to see that the sky is you, your inner Self. You are above the fog and you are not affected by things you defined your life by in the past. Though thoughts and mental fabrications will rise and fall as they always do, you will not rise and fall with them. You will transcend them by being the sky. Having a "sky like nature of mind," of being, as the Buddha said, releases you from the cage of form.

Life is not a fight, it is a miracle.

You are the sky, beyond definition, beyond conceptualization.

You are nothing and yet you are everything.

Smile at this realization and let go:

Today you shine from Self,

Today you shine for all.

Nature

"The color of the mountain is Buddha's body; the
sound of running water is his great speech"
                                    - Zen Master Dogen

"Nature is what we know
Yet have not the art to say,
So impotent our wisdom is to her simplicity."
                                    - Emily Dickinson

"Every day, priests minutely examine the Dharma
And endlessly chant complicated sutras.
Before doing that, though, they should learn
How to read the love letters sent by the wind and rain, the
snow and moon"
                                    - Zen Master Ikkyu

If one wishes to deepen into the Self, he or she can aid the process through developing a connection with nature. Nature is graceful, wild, and intricately layered – beyond the scope of imagination or conceptualization. It is powerful. It is everywhere, all the time, and it encompasses all things, including us. Letting go of our daily bustling schedule and going into nature represents a form of surrender to the one organism from which we sprung. We relinquish the apparent foregrounds of our lives to go into a deeper place that has no plan – it just is. Nature is the reflection of what we are below our thoughts. Having more appreciation for the earth, and the things our logical mind might deem 'simple' or 'boring' – a soft light, the sounds of birds in a forest, or the texture of a weathered path – strengthens our ability to inhabit the now and respect what is. Appreciating the ordinary – *the natural things* – and being open and present enough to appreciate it, deepens us and turns us toward reverence for the myriad aspects of *this* one experience.

It is important to find time in our weekly schedules to let go and get out. We must leave our limited and conceptual "yards" to touch the unfolding, unknowable nature of the world. There is so much moving around us all the time without our consent or our manipulation. Life is flowing whether we want it to or not – whether we agree with it or not. The earth is a pulsating web that we can connect with. And we are connected.[77] Oftentimes our feelings of loneliness or disconnection stem from our inability to be in touch with the world around us. We become cut off and stuck in a little subjective bubble our ego has created. Our problems, our desires, our selfish attitudes, and our busy minds affect our way of seeing the world. We no longer experience an ancient, universal connection to what we have come from, nature, but instead we look to contemporary falsehoods. This is a fundamental observation, and it is an interesting one to examine. When we become obsessed with our own creation stories or transfixed by a gadget or machine, then something deep and vibrant is missing. When we come to nature and we are willing to let go of who we think we are as well as the small things we attach ourselves to, nature gives us the opportunity to see right through and step into vastness. It could be a wonderful and yet simple move to reconnect with the fundamental flow that gives us life.

The natural world offers us refuge from the unrelenting ego while allowing us to see what manifests on its own without small mind. The cycles of life, birth and death and flood and drought, continue without any thoughts or internal transgressions. We often believe that we control what is happening all the time. We think that to lose control is a bad thing. Sit down, let go, and see how nature takes care of things perfectly, without the toils of the small mind. Also, see your place, your essential equality with all things in the face of this reality. Nature does not judge you as rich, poor, black, white, brown, important, or unimportant. It welcomes you as you are and if you can get in touch with this, you might learn to embody the natural attitude of total acceptance. The 'thusness' of nature – its ability to be free from thought or logic – allows it to flow perfectly into balance. We can learn something from this.[78]

Over the years I have experienced some of my deepest moments observing, interacting, and sitting with nature. Hooting owls, journeying butterflies, curious dolphins, and even an excited, howling pack of wolves have made their way into my life and shifted something within my mind. And then there is the scenery, beautiful sunsets that are never quite the same, and the countless gleaming stars at night, too, breaking down the walls of an attitude or emotion that had confined me to smallness. These sights, as well as the sound of crashing waves or the cackling of a fire, are primordial experiences that go beyond thinking, speaking, or even chanting. Even a passing robin or the pattering of rain on dry gravel reveals its own kind of depth that is beyond anything I could ever make, think, or do, and this is an intriguing thing to notice.

> It is said that a monk once asked an old Zen master how he should enter into the Way. The master replied and asked the monk if he could hear the faint sound of a rushing stream nearby, and the monk said that he could. The master told the monk, "Enter there!"

Through sitting in nature I found that breathing and listening represent the language of wisdom, which we can all experience even more acutely and profoundly through the simple gesture of being present with the earth. There is so much to be found, and at the same time lost, within letting go and unfurling into the natural.

Nature was and still is a refuge for me. As I moved along my path, I often went out on long hikes to remove myself from the bustling world. No more news, sports, social issues, family, just my original roots – reaching into the fabric of what is here. I was consciously walking away from a smaller kind of 'life' to give myself the space to be with what truly is, to see what I am made of, and also, integrally a part of. Walking, being, smelling, witnessing, and letting go: I could lose much of 'who' I thought I was.[79] Like meditation, a walk in the woods takes time from our busy lives. There were moments when I had to use effort to push myself to go out and leave daily business behind. But like meditation, too, nature also gives back much more than what we put in: perspective, balance, and wholeness – all of which come from connecting to one's Self. What other treasures are there to receive than this?

> Stepping into the unknown wilderness, clearing the mind of old habits and endless thought – this is nature.

There is nothing quite like sitting on top of a mountain and watching the fog interweave through twisting valleys below. A splintered tree, a cracked cliff face, and an unending forest nourish us when we are receptive enough to receive them. As we continue to open, to see, to appreciate, we are steadier and ready to witness the small blessings that surround us throughout the motion of daily life. We come back to our man-made world a little more balanced, a little more connected to something beyond the cityscape. Someone may ask, "Are you ok? You seem a little stoic, a little calmer today…" We may even ask if we are ok. I know I still do this. It seems strange, even a little bizarre at first. Life is opening and we are losing a part of who we thought we were, maybe more quickly than we had originally expected. Even our minds are a little bit more tired today. "Is this ok?" we ask. Yes, things are moving inside and we are opening up, going beyond our old perceptions and opinions, our little bubble bobbing among the waves.

> Most importantly, nature allows us to be with ourselves. We are removed from society, but in this removal, we must be willing to see within; not thoughts or projections, but what lies beneath – our true nature.

In the Preface I mentioned keys. Nature can provide us with the keys necessary to open the doors within. A mountain bluebird, a delicate flower, a soaring hawk, or the sound of the wind moving among the redwood trees can slam into us and crack into our ego's walls. A fog bank clears, revealing a perfect sky or an illuminated mountainside, and suddenly we become free. We are removed from our small mind, our ego, and we are able to step through the doorway. Everything becomes clear, the seemingly huge wave-like issues disappear, and we settle into the present moment. There is nothing to fear, nothing to hide from. The earth is here and we are part of the earth, wrapped in the midst of infinity. These are just glimpses, small experiences, but they have the power to unlock the doors of the mind. The more of these experiences we digest, the more exposed we are to truth. This exposure, these brief moments of egoic death, give space for the Self to arise.

> The temple is there. There is only one question. The question is, "Can we see it?"

Nature allows us to see ourselves in a humble way. When we bend down and touch the earth, we are giving the natural world, our home, respect. In this respect lies our appreciation for life and our acceptance of our place within the infinite universe. The earth is our oyster. It has given us existence.[80] It is our home and our mother, and from what we scientifically know, there is nothing like it – it truly is a miracle. We live because the earth lives and we thrive because the earth thrives. When we cannot understand this, we are blind and wrapped in a fog – we are foolishly taking our existence for granted.

Nature also reflects our inner being because nature is. We can achieve the same oneness when we look around at what is before us. Our inner nature mirrors this dynamic.[81] When we consciously go out into nature, we are removing ourselves from our Selves. How much we judge ourselves, how hard we are on ourselves is shown to us when we are in nature. It is pure, it is neutral – it is the undistorted mirror. What we make of it reflects who we are in this moment and where we are, mentally, in this moment. When we are not present and when we become lost in thoughts, nature is there. Through being in nature – watching, witnessing, remaining alert, and letting go of who we are – our true *nature* becomes evident.

The natural world is like a *koan*: an ancient Zen saying, phrase, or short dialogue used by masters to pry open the minds of neophyte disciples. The power of the koan lies in its ability to work on the individual, not the other way around. A koan is used to deconstruct, to bring our created worlds crashing down, and to add insult to injury (for the ego), burning them away into nothingness. Once the disciple is opened and flayed out, the koan settles, and the disciple discerns its true meaning. Nature can become our physical koan. It has the power to connect us to something far beyond the confines of our small minds, and the ability to take down our created mental walls, to let us walk without defense – to be centered and rooted. Everything we need can be found within the forests, among the mountains, under the crags, and in the oceans. When we can get in touch with this reality, we are getting in touch with what we are.

> Life is here already, all around us.
> Do we feel it? Are we ready to see through?
> The keys are there.
> We must become the doors.
> Feeling this, turning in
> Is our way.

We are connected and we are the ones who must wake up to this truth. Practice takes time, but we know this, we are budding practitioners.

Find the profound lessons nature offers us. Sit underneath a tree. Stand by a rushing stream. Watch an egret move among the reeds. Listen and tap into something that is beyond anything we could ever consume or dream up. We can learn so much from these things. Wisdom, the flow of life, and patience are three gems we can find right here in nature. Nature can cleanse our souls and it can uplift our spirits. To appreciate nature is such a simple and basic thing. Yet, many of us think that we do not have the capability to sit and truly witness this miracle that is around us all the time. We are too preoccupied with fantasy scenarios of the mind to be able to sit and enjoy our Eden. How can we be true to ourselves if we cannot sit and be?

The Spectrum of Darkness & Light

"During the night, Te-shan entered Master Lung-t'an's room and stood in attendance till late at night.

Lung-t'an said, "Why don't you go?

Te-shan bade farewell and went out; he saw that it was dark outside, so he turned around and said, "It's dark outside."

Lung-t'an lit a paper lantern and handed it to Te-shan; as soon as Te-shan took it, Lung-t'an blew it out.

Te-shan was vastly and greatly enlightened."

We often categorize our experiences into good or bad, exciting or boring, traumatizing or enriching. "The candy tasted great, I am happy." "The man was angry with me, I am upset." And as we move along, life swings back and forth between the poles. But what if what we think of as bad, negative, uncomfortable, or a waste of time is actually something meaningful and worthwhile – an opportunity for growth, a key to unlocking something within ourselves? What if we could feel or experience something deeper, beyond what we are comfortable with presently, when we are able to drop our likes and aversions, our ideas of darkness and light, to realize an open mind?

Wading into our discomforts as well as the incalculable and uncontrollable reality we are a part of is what makes us grow. It is the alchemy of realization – of going into the darkness without the comforting flashlight of our thoughts, beliefs, and rigid opinions. Master Lung-t'an's kind and creative teaching struck down Te-shan's beliefs. He took Te-shan's small mind, the lantern, and gave him the entire universe in return through the simple extinguishment of his expectations. It was within the darkness that Te-shan awakened, not the light and this is the key. When we open this example up, sit with it intimately, and bring it into our lives, we find that our own growth can come from being in the darkness of the unknown and letting go of our habitual responses.

If, before we begin our practice, we experience life as a spectrum of good and bad moments we perceive and judge, then the spectrum can also be viewed as one of light and darkness, darkness and light. Everything that comes and everything we feel is placed upon it, depending on where we wish to place them. When we remove ourselves through practice, this spectrum disappears, and what is, is – without labels. The present is just watched and experienced, and in the grand scheme of things, everything is totally accepted. This state of permeability, Hakuin's equanimity, is where we are headed. But for now, we are still here. We are James, Amy, Erica, John, Don, Alex, Max, Haley, and Molly. We have just learned to expand ourselves and to see the ordinary, what we might call 'grey,' as remarkable.

Going beyond the ease of light and the neutrality of the ordinary, then, what about the dark and negative *feelings?* The moments of anger, fear, depression, resentment, jealousy, pride, and detachment – the feelings we do not want to visit? They are the phantoms we keep at bay: the ones lurking below the surface, sitting hand-in-hand with the causes that spurred their arrival. We don't pay attention to them, we shun them, and so they live, ignored within the depths of who we are. They are not gone. They are with us all the time, whether we are aware of them or not, just below the surface. They rear their heads in the form of addiction, irresponsible behavior, defensive walls, impulsive reactions, avoidance, aversion, unending thought streams, and social masks – things of which we can remain completely unconscious. Neglecting our dark regions perpetuates our unconsciousness, keeping us from being able to transcend the ego. It is important to become real and to feel these states consciously when they appear – not to avoid them or comply with them. All we must do is watch and remain attentive. There is power in this activity. Some of the 'greatest' men have gone out to conquer because they could not conquer themselves. Conquering others was the easy way out, their excuse for not dealing with their inner movements. Facing our demons, when we are ready, is the most pure and courageous action we can undertake.

What about the dark *moments or events* – a death, a hurtful phone call, an impending diagnosis? How about the loss of a friendship, the pain of a fall, the sight of people suffering, the destruction of a forest, or the wailing of a neglected child? These things happen. Our lives move into these events, and in turn, these events move into us. We react through the building of a new inner wall for our fortress, or we judge in order to remove ourselves from the pain. It seems so right to do because it involves our ego's survival. Completely accepting these moments and practicing to sit with them, fully aware, is very difficult and painful. Why be exposed to such things? Why feel such things? They are dark and frightening, part of the unknown wilderness in which we do not wish to tread. We want to protect ourselves by closing off and avoiding them. We call the dark moments 'bad moments' and we want nothing to do with them. This is understandable. But is it living, is it right? Are we growing? Are we, in a sense, running from our Selves? To tread consciously through the muck is to transcend the muck and to find the pearl within it. Oftentimes these pearls – these moments of utter freedom – become the most beautiful, rewarding gems we can ever uncover.

> "When one door of happiness closes, another opens; but often we look so long at the closed door that we do not see the one that has been opened for us."
>
> – Helen Keller

It may take time, but patience and steady consciousness always provide, because life provides. We are just waking up to it. There is always life, always an opportunity buried within the 'darkness' we perceive. But in order to find it, we must be the open vessel ready to receive it. Sometimes the greatest shifts within, the most powerful keys, come buried within darkness. The near-death experience brings new eyes. The experiencer, once on his deathbed, runs through the streets, thankful for each and every second of life. "Phew, that was close!" she exclaims. The man on the edge of breaking down loses control and cries. Everything he has ever known falls apart. He lies in a heap on the floor, he has just lost everything. He is a broken man. Is that so? Are we broken when this happens, or is something else going on? Begin shifting your perception of where good comes from and where bad comes from, and whether the two are really separate categorical entities.

My life transformed when I felt some sort of bottom. Some part of me fell away when I hit the ground and I was ok with it. Rather than continuing my habits and searching for something outside, I just sat with the passing and I let it be. New life sprang forth with a certain quality – one of appreciation and depth. Also, I am continually tested, like all of us, each day. Do I fail? Of course, and that is ok. It is called getting up off of the ground – the same ground I have fallen upon – and it is the most necessary part of my growth.[82] An internal shift is a beautiful thing to realize and experience and it cannot come unless I-you-we are down on the ground, flayed out, awake, ready to greet the coming guest.

The darkness provides the light a medium to exist, It gives

the light a brilliance it might not have otherwise had, without the contrast.

We can run from the dark as much as we want, but in doing so, we are running from an even greater light, and thus an opportunity for awakening or rebirth. We know that change and death bring new life in the natural world. Why does this law not apply to consciousness – to our inner realms in *this life, right now*? Is it because it doesn't apply, or is it because we have not yet been able to see it?

While going into the dark regions, the unknown and also the uncomfortable, represent the highest and consequently the most difficult forms of inner transformation, we can aid the process – strengthening ourselves – by enjoying and remaining present during the seemingly mundane moments in our day-to-day lives. Learning to see the majesty within the ordinary is a solid first step toward accepting and inhabiting the present because most of our lives are filled with such moments. A butterfly, the lighting on the front porch, a dog scampering after a tennis ball, or the sound of raindrops on the bus windshield can all enrich our experience of daily life. They are keys for us to discover and, consequently, they may have the power to open us.

There is an inherent 'thusness' within the ordinary that can shine through our created walls. Training ourselves to enjoy the regular sights, the mundane movements, and to see the beauty interwoven within ordinariness enhances our total experience. But most significantly, when we accept the unacceptable – *when we realize that what we don't expect or want might be the avenue for our own aw-*

akening, then life takes on a new texture we could not have imagined otherwise.[83] We don't know what will open us, thus we remain open to each and *every* moment.

We must greet the bright day and the long night as we would old, tired friends.[84] One sight, one sound, the autumn wind, a break-up, or our own broken reflection on the ripples of a pond, can shift us into a new state of being. The more we expose ourselves to the darker moments in life – the unknown or what makes us uncomfortable – without the protection of our internal armor, our comforting opinions and justifications, the more we will inevitably shift into being. We can deepen further because we are experiencing more and more *without* our created version of reality. This is living 100 percent. We are opening to life and life mirrors our opening. It is that simple. But once again, we must be the ones willing to open our doors, inch by inch, diligently and patiently.

> Our darker moments, the unpleasant and challenging ones, become interesting – something to experience and something to examine. There is a texture, a kind of marrow for inner growth that we will miss if we shun the unknown.

There is so much for us to work with every day. Every second is a moment to remain present, every sensation is a feeling to feel, and every event is one to experience – to see through and to accept. When we experience this, life becomes a giant opportunity for practice, and we are increasingly here to meet it as it is. A fundamental shift will occur within us if we are conscious enough to 'stay awake,' especially while passing through our painful moments.

> Are we willing to work with it?[85] Are we willing to go beyond our small yards and broaden, expanding to encompass the full 360-degree, three-dimensional sphere of it all? It is in our hands. The choice is ours.

The more we view the ordinary experiences as something to cherish, the more we enrich our lives.[86] The simple, moving-along moments fill our days. They are neutral and so are we. We are driving, we are walking to get lunch, we are sitting watching the television, we are spacing out, but when we turn off the TV, when we walk mindfully and we remain alert, we begin to see the flux around us. We see all that is before us moving in a dance. We are more open to catching a glimpse of the passing songbird, the kind gesture, the laughing girl eating her melting ice cream cone. Even the sun passing through the trees can bring a feeling of warmth that lasts throughout the day and into the night. Everything flows so naturally, and it is all so full of life. There is an undeniable intimacy that can be felt. Don't miss out on it by being stuck in a fictitious world – one we are trying to fight for and control. There is a whole reality outside our walls waiting to be experienced. Wisdom comes from our ability to drink from the richness of life.

> Begin to see the beautiful within the ordinary. You will expand out from your bubble and you will enrich your life naturally. Being present, watchful, and mindful of our state

of mind, we open the door to our own world. We are truly giving and receiving at all times, breath after breath, sight after sight. Be aware of this and witness what is manifesting around us constantly.

We have options in each given now. We can go to the bottle, we can deny, we can over-work and avoid, we can remain unconscious, or we can face what comes and patiently move through it. The situation is still heavy, but there is space and within that space, that emptiness, lays the seed of our awakening, or of a new, deep understanding. When we still the mind and we sit with what is, there is a natural healing process. We are surrendering and we are feeling. What was once so daunting remains, but with time, it begins to lift. We are breathing, we are feeling, we are completely aware of everything and eventually what once was moves on. If we stay in meditation, we open the door for wisdom to come. When we go out into the world, we are more open genuinely to life and life is more open to us. It is all about being with everything. Being right here, right now, with the dark and the light – the whole – conscious and aware, mindful of what is happening on the inside and the outside, is what practicing is all about.[87]

It takes practice. Seeing the beautiful in the ordinary is the first step. Being honest with ourselves, facing our demons and finding the pearls within the darkness, steadies our pace toward deeper consciousness. It is not the easiest thing, but it is wonderful and real.

Blow Down the Walls

A Zen koan says,

"If you turn things around, you are like the Buddha."

The koan is straightforward and direct: turn things around, be Buddhas. Within the now, there is nothing standing in our way. An awakened individual, a Buddha, a master turns things around until there is simply nothing left – no borders, no sense of direction or distinction between east and west, not even a mental map to use as a tool to formulate ideas about who we think we are and what we should do.[88] There are no walls or obstructions to block the flow of what naturally comes and what naturally goes, rather, all that remains is wide-open space. Turning things around flips our mental fortresses upside down and allows us to enter into an entirely new way of living. That is the heart of this koan. Some can invert their entire lives in an instant, embracing space and all things as one. And others, like me, root into practice and turn over the myriad internal walls one at a time.

I remember sitting with "turn things around" out on the bluffs by Santa Barbara. The monarch butterflies were on their annual migration up the coast meandering through the Eucalyptus trees, landing on sun-dipped branches and dodging spider webs. Their lives played out in this way among the shifting breeze, and so did the life I was experiencing. Under the same sun, cancer scares, car accidents, financial troubles, laughter, the Golden Gate Bridge, foggy mornings and starry nights, dirty dishes, football games, and my thoughts unfolded along the path: the substances and the moments comprising *this* migration or journey on which I had somehow embarked. Nothing had changed, life was still made of calming sun streaks and challenging, sticky webs, and I was increasingly here to greet the inexhaustible fluctuations between the two, while learning to seize up less. There was a quality, an intimacy growing that I could only experience through my Self. Attempting to convey my experience to others manifested in the form of evocative words and slicing hand gestures – missing the mark, yet refreshing and humorous at times.[89]

> Falling down on the ground, standing up again, pausing a little longer each time, to notice, to see my inner Self in the endless ripples and countless reflections.

I also remember speaking to an elder Zen teacher over green tea and Mexican cuisine (a prototypical California-style meal) about his more than thirty years of Zen practice. He said, "The real question is, what will you do when the man raises his middle finger, or the woman is screaming? Where is your Zen practice then?" He smiled, with a look of seriousness. The aromas, the sound of dishes clattering and people chatting, melded with his words and gave them a texture of sorts, a practical significance that went hand-in-hand with what it means to live mindfully. There was life in these words, an echoing that reverberated throughout the room and harkened back to ancient times. His question is a deeply Buddhist one – where is your practice when times are hard, when suddenly you meet a giant, over-powering wave? For me, and for the sake of this book, turning things around and transforming into the ocean seemed like an appropriate answer. When we can take a contentious, seething moment or an unrelenting desire and invert it on itself, then this is Buddha's practice. The elderly Zen teacher's words continue to ring out today, too, emanating from the brown table on which I write, the flock of parrots that has made its home a few blocks from mine, and the truck climbing up the steep grade below the fire escape. There wasn't a perfect answer for the teacher's words at that moment, only a spontaneous nod, an acceptance of not having the answers and being comfortable with that. Challenges will come, and so will middle fingers, but Buddha's practice remains Buddha's practice. Inhabiting the now and remaining centered through what comes is turning things around.

I notice how the sum of my narrow perspectives forms the comfortable walls within which I enclose myself, causing me to lose touch with what is here. When I attempt to turn things around within my mind, I work to blow down the walls and step into fresh, open space, allowing life to unfold just as it is. And this is what I ask you to look into, to attempt, when the time comes or when it just feels right. Each maneuver, each crumbling of our barriers brings us closer to a clear vision of reality and the selfless, balanced characteristics that come with such a view. This represents the ultimate freedom – one that is necessary for a transformation of heart and mind.

The Vision: The Self – complete consciousness in the now

The Way: Turning in and cultivating a daily practice

The Mantra: Mindfulness, awareness, and acceptance of what is

The whole purpose behind the words within this text lies in the seemingly mundane, self-help-style title, *see for your Self.* It is a mirror for us to examine ourselves, to witness the 'who' you and I have created, and to begin tearing down the images and projections we have made about the world we move through. As I said in the Preface, there is no teacher here, just the beginning of a conversation, and the imparting of something that may or may not push you, the reader, into a different kind of experience, a brand new arena of consciousness. Going into meditation, looking into other Zen works, and expanding our horizons opens up our inner avenues for a soulful and spiritual change.

Come back six months from now and look at some of the chapters. If you have practiced witnessing, your interpretations of the words expressed here might be different and fresh. Maybe the text will have become dull and your interpretations will crunch right through my words! Or maybe you will find new meaning in a line that seemed as ordinary as a wisp of cloud. If you are sincere in your practice, you move on, and if you gaze deeply into the nature of life with an increasingly quieted mind, you deepen. Life, and all the ordinary moments it comprises, becomes more and more beautiful and you become increasingly here to reap the benefits of experiencing life just as it is.

No matter what we go through, we must always remain open. A path can lose its power and its ability to renew and refresh when we become blind followers. Any form of mindfulness is a wonderful framework, but at some point along the road, we must be courageous enough to claim our own sovereignty, to realize the Self and then to move beyond the framework. It is not something to fear, but something to rejoice in. This is the essence of turning the light of our consciousness inwards.[90]

Remember, the Buddha was represented or symbolized by footprints for hundreds of years before he was finally shaped into a statue for worship.[91] Remember, too, when a Zen master famously proclaimed, "Kill the Buddha!" that the goal of practice is to realize your Self, not to emulate someone other than *You*! Not to do or be anything else. We follow the framework for years. We continue to practice as a way of life, meditating and remaining mindful and aware each and every day. But in the end, we must take ownership of our paths, when we fall down, when we stand up, when we are walking, and when we are sitting on the groundless ground.[92]

Buddha referred to himself as a physician not a philosopher. He doesn't tell us about what light or emptiness is, he helps us see it on our own. Then he moves on and leaves us to our own devices. In the Diamond Sutra, Buddha (Tathagata) told his most faithful disciple, Subhuti:

> "What do you think, Subhuti, does it occur to a Tathagata, 'by me have beings been set free?' Not thus should you see it Subhuti! And why? There is not any being whom the Tathagata has set free. Those who by my form did see me, and those who followed me by voice, wrong were the efforts they engaged in."

We are already free, sentient, conscious beings. It is our true nature. In his words, the Buddha does not come as our savior or as a forgiving God. He comes to tell us what we are missing for ourselves; what we cannot see or experience through the glossy haze we perpetuate. There is nothing to gain, nothing to understand, just an essence to realize and actualize.[93] Buddha is telling us not to imitate him our whole lives, because to do so is to miss the mark completely.[94] We must be the ones to transcend teaching, to free ourselves through the direct experience of turning things around on our own, moment after moment. It is just a matter of whether or not we are willing to wake from our dream of separateness and see reality as it is in the now.[95] That is the view of Buddhas – who we are – and it comes through the practice of unpeeling and unpeeling and unpeeling the layers of ego. I am still unpeeling, going through what feels right, what feels wrong and what feels completely upside down. I trudge through the mud and muck, too, of old, painful abuses and current conflicts, but I can feel the texture on my toes. This is intriguing, and just as much a part of my path as any other precious moment.

It is empowering to know that we are our own doors, our own individual passageways to freedom. But that is not always enough. Waking up and walking through is just the beginning. Continuing down our roads becomes our way of being in this world, but not to be totally of it – not to be tossed about by the waves coming forward and then receding into the background. There is a fine balance between the pure words of all the Buddhas and the day-to-day things that challenge us. The path is learning to find that balance.

Each step brings more consciousness. Each moment is another gem to touch and experience. We are taking matters into our own hands, bringing the light of awareness to the world and ourselves wherever we go. Whether it is on the meditation cushion or emanating from the latte, the keys for our growing awareness abound. We are slowly transcending the dream and grounding into reality. We are learning to be *here* each and every moment in life, and that is a gift – the gift. We are learning to touch others, to reach down into our inner Self, and care for the earth on which we tread every moment. And one day, something clicks. We may look at a tree covered in light and laugh at such a simple, profound sight – laughing and laughing our way into the night.[96]

Blow down the walls and see for your Self.

Daily Practices & Recognition

"Be content with what you have; rejoice in the way things are. When you realize there is nothing lacking, the whole world belongs to you."

- Zen proverb

"Whenever you study and ask questions, there aren't so many things to be concerned with. Concerns arise because *outside* you perceive that mountains and rivers and the great earth exists; *within* you perceive that seeing, hearing, feeling, and knowing exist; *above* you see that there are various buddhas that can be sought; and *below* you see that there are sentient beings who can be saved. You must simply spit them all out at once: afterwards, whether walking, standing, sitting, or lying down, twenty-four hours a day, you fuse everything into one. Then, though you are on the tip of a hair, it's as broad as the universe"

-Yuan Wu, The Blue Cliff Record

The following visualizations and practices are meant to encourage you to begin cultivating a practice. Some may have dabbled in meditation and some may have not. Sitting in silence can be very difficult, but it is also necessary for one to turn in and reach toward the Self. Though I recommend diving head first into silent meditation and koan practice, these visualizations will help slow us down if we are not ready for a formal practice. Through the subsequent examples, we begin to unpeel the layers of small mind and wade out into vastness.

Visualizations

1. Conscious Gardening

Close your eyes and take a few deep breaths. Feel the in-breath reaching down into your loins. Slowly exhale and release any tension in the body. Concentrate on the breath and stare deeply into the blackness before you. Allow any thoughts just to flow through. Do not attach to them. Just let them float by. Do this for a few moments until you are relaxed and centered. Now, imagine yourself getting into an old elevator. See your hand reach out to press the down button and then watch the doors close before you. Watch the numbers slowly count down from ten to one with each breath cycle (inhalation and exhalation). With each number, feel yourself falling deeper and deeper into the recesses of your mind, into the infinite blackness of your subconscious. Three … Two… One. The elevator stops and the doors open. Before you lies a patch of the most fertile soil. It is a sponge shrouded in fog and mist. Smile at this sight for it is the dormant field of your dreams. All the potential in the world is right in front of your very nose. This is your garden. You are the gardener and it is time to plant the seeds of life that you wish to cultivate – joy, love, harmony, and health. Reach down and begin your gardening with mindfulness. Place each seed in its hole and calmly cover it with soil. Feel its texture. See the space between each planting, space that is necessary for growth. The damp, rich soil in combination with your thoughts of nourishment will only speed its manifestation. Spend time in your subconscious garden and make sure that you continue to be fully present in the here and now. Now come back and smile at what you have just achieved. Go about your day in mindfulness. Be present in your activities fully and your seeds of life will flourish.

2. Inner Strength

Sit down and relax. Breath in and out several times, slowly. Allow everything to wash from your body like the tide leaving the seashore. Now close your eyes. Each breath cleanses the soul and replenishes the spirit. Focus on the breath and let everything fade. After three to four minutes, begin to envision a ball of light in your lower stomach. Allow it to grow slowly until it encompasses you in a golden orb. Feel your pulse and let it rhythmically merge with the light.

3. Enhancing Your Presence

Close your eyes and take three deep, slow breaths in and out through your nose and mouth. Take a few moments to relax and settle into your meditative state of calm. When you have reached this level, raise your arms out in front of your body and open your palms as wide as you can. Continue to breathe and begin to feel the pulse of your body, the pulse of your internal energy that sustains you each moment. Give thanks to this internal, life-giving energy, and then place your awareness fully into your outstretched palms. Breathe into your palms. Give them all the life energy that you have collected, and see this energy in the form of balls of light resting in your hands. Let the light energy grow with each mindful, concentrated breath. Slowly begin to move your outstretched palms back and forth, creating a transparent field of light before you. Strengthen this field through continued mindfulness and visualization. Delve into it fully and feel that this field is always within you – it is you. Let it settle around you for a few moments. When you return, know what you have created and have faith that it is there always.

4. I Am Buddha

Sit or lie down and close your eyes. Breathe, clear your mind of everything, and step into the present. After you have established yourself in the now, see the enlightened Buddha sitting in the lotus position under the Bodhi tree. Concentrate on his face. He is calm, he is at peace, he is beyond mind and beyond self. His very being is a power that cannot be described – just experienced through you. See this image so clearly that it moves you, rattling your mind. Drink Buddha's presence. Slowly allow this image to come towards you… Buddha is right in front of you. His energy field reverberates throughout your body. Make space in yourself for the Buddha and let his image merge with yours. The Buddha is now you.

You are the Buddha.

Let this realization seep in fully. Your mind is sky, your body is earth, your being is now. Thoughts are nothing but ghosts that dissipate in the steady breeze of your presence. For your presence is vastness. Feel it all. Take it all in, breath after miraculous breath. Let your intention be *right*, your speech *impeccable*, your action in the *here and now*, and your character *solid*.

5. Walking Within the Web

As you prepare for your day, do so mindfully. When you shower, shower. When you eat, eat. When you read the paper, read the paper. It seems simple, but as you know, it requires discipline. This sets the tone for the day. Stopping and deeply planting some intentions is also good, but when you are done and you have watered them, let them go and head out. As you walk, imagine a translucent chord shooting out of your body and into whatever object or person you are moving toward. There is no need to look. It is just a way of being, of knowing your place within the grand scheme. Begin by just connecting with what comes. As it passes, let it go and see the next object of your attention. As before, let it come and let it go. As with thoughts in meditation, objects, things we perceive, come and go. Allow them to be, give them space, respect, and let them pass by. You are completely here on your walk, seeing life as it is. With time, you will be able to send more chords out, more pieces of web. This not only increases your connection to all things, but your openness, your presence, and your light as well.

Practices

1. Power Word Practice

Something that aided me when I began turning in was creating a board of power words. I would pick three or four words each day and I would focus on thinking and acting in a way that reflected the values on the list. The Six Paramitas (the six practices that lead to enlightenment) are practiced by those who call themselves Bodhisattvas. A Bodhisattva is the ultimate compassionate and selfless being. The Six Paramitas represent a Bodhisattva's daily commitment to this altruistic goal.

> Generosity
>
> Discipline
>
> Patience
>
> Diligence
>
> Meditation
>
> Wisdom

Consciously planting these seeds in the mind through mindfulness and daily practice will bring peace to you as well as those who come in contact with you.

2. The Gadget-less practice

The gadget-less practice allowed me to be more present while increasing my level of self-awareness. How often do we go to our phone to send a text, make a call, or go on the Internet when nothing is going on? What about music, the computer, TV, the game system, or some other electronic? Every time we are bored we impulsively run to these devices to kill time, to remain separate from ourselves. Knowing this and removing such devices from our lives when we can allows us to learn to be with what is: the present moment and the Self. Truly being with what is, right here, right now, we are free from the cycles. An inherent joy settles and life is beautiful as it is.

Give yourself the space to see, to be reality by consciously removing the things that keep you from realization. It should become a daily practice, especially for those of us who rely heavily on electronics throughout the day. Let them go, and be. Then, when the time comes, come back to daily life with what you have felt. Life will appear different. Peace, balance, and equanimity will naturally ensue.

3. The Silence Practice

Silence allows space in the context of a noisy mind. Take time throughout the day to be silent and still. I was amazed at how much my concentration and my presence increased by just listening to the sounds of life outside my head. When the world is crumbling, i.e. there is traffic on the freeway, be silent and witness life in the here and now. As we watch objectively, life begins to flow exactly as it is supposed to. By being silent you change nothing but your point of view. Suddenly, this traffic jam becomes an opportunity to breathe and be.

4. The Gratitude Practice

Gratitude increases our acceptance of what is. "Thank you universe for everything. Thank you for life, consciousness, health…" Through being thankful and appreciative, we send out a signal, a frequency of positive energy. Life responds to this. No matter how dark our life situation is, right here, right now, there is light. Find that light and send it gratitude. By just finding the light and consciously sending it thanks, you plant the seed of change. In the morning, your eyes will be that much more open to catch the glimmer of the sun shinning through a hole in the fog. Stay in gratitude and life will respond.

Epilogue

An old master said,

> "The great *Way* is not difficult
> If you just don't pick and choose"
> - Sengcan (Seng-ts'an)

The open mind is one that is like a metaphorical sky: vast to the point of laughter, clear, and accepting of the various storm (thought) systems and cloud formations appearing and disappearing below. There isn't a notion to change anything, just a witnessing and a being that flow with the naturalness of the moment. It could be an interesting experience to step into the realm of openness, putting down picking and choosing, likes and dislikes, and leaving the life of small storm systems to inhabit largeness. There might be something luscious about stepping into what is occurring as it is.

Picking and choosing implies a kind of limitation of sorts between what is – reality – and what the mind desires to see and strives to attain. There can be resistance, aversion, defensiveness, manipulation, and a sheep-like tendency to follow others, streaming out of a decision made from the unexamined, ego-based mind without us ever realizing it. And there is conflict here too, one in which an infinitesimally small subject mentally pushes against a perceived outer, infinite object, when in reality they are both part of an overarching oneness. Stepping into this oneness might come from the simple, mindful practice of being ok with what is: cancer, chocolate, deceased pets, work, sandy toes, hawks, and of course, traffic!

The koan written above originates from an old Zen master named Sengcan, an almost mythical figure or wild-man who roamed China's wilderness sometime between the first and sixth centuries. It's fun to watch scholars try to pin Sengcan down to a certain place or time, as if he meant to be a reclusive hermit for eternity not to be a nuisance, but to be more like a continually surviving and humorous teaching or practical joke. As if within his leaping into the shadows of the unknown is a hidden and yet straightforward teaching meant to say, "Stop trying to find me through history! Put down your discerning mind and step into the moment right now... Oh, how nice it is to meet you!" In the Zen tradition he is viewed as one of the original Patriarchs, and for the sake of this book we'll let him rest there for now.

When I bring Sengcan's koan, "The great Way is not difficult if you just don't pick and choose," into *this* life, I am often struck by its ability to break down my internal walls, allowing more of the texture of life to seep into my awareness. Something that may have dissuaded me before becomes an opportunity to enjoy the moment in a new way, and I am able to expand from the fortress of the 'who' that I think I am. I also notice how things begin to have a spacious quality or lightness to them when I don't have the urge to pick or choose my opinions about how the moment should be. It's not that the external event, the world, or even the universe is different — how could that ever be possible? It's my interaction with what is and my perception of what is that has changed.[1]

There is also a joyful sense of playfulness wrapped within Sengcan's words: when faced with a decision between cake or pie, I might decide in that moment, "redwood!" blowing up my small mind and opening a door towards a kind of internal freedom or vastness I would otherwise not have been able to experience. Maybe this opening of the mind is the lusciousness, the thusness of life I have often read about in books, unfurling into *this* direct experience of the world and the moment, here, now.

Not picking and choosing includes all things, entering into the realms I fear and keep at bay, the real storms that block me from knowing my own sky-like nature. Sickness, being alone, past grievances, anger and grief, and the greatest teacher of all, death, are all intimate parts of the totality of experience that I *choose* to ignore and fend off. Allowing the koan to settle in these instances within my life removes a kind of seething, underlying resistance that slithers below my perception of the world. When this subtle uneasiness is removed, then what is, is free to be as it is, and it takes on a natural brilliance on its own, without having to fit into my narrow, prescribed view of how things should be. And so, there might be a transformative experience waiting to be directly realized within not picking and choosing.

---

[1] It could be an intriguing idea to step into no-perception. And instead of labeling, it might be an expansive move to see the apparent individual moments in life as... life!

Here is a story about a Welsh grandmother's passing and the naturalness of not picking and choosing in the face of the greatest kind of transformation, leaving this life and moving into the unknown wilderness.

A Welsh grandmother was passing away from lung cancer and the annual pilgrimage of windswept fall leaves. There wasn't anything that could be done and she knew deeply that the end of her path was near, whether she wanted it to be or not. As the disease progressed, she watched her family come and go through the bedroom door, giving her blessings and longing "I love you's." Her dutiful old dog, Tess, her husband of forty-five years clucking about the room like a worried mother hen, her son and granddaughter flown all the way from sunny San Diego, and her frowning sister: each brought his or her own unique flavor of love and care that was tantalizing to the senses.

She had never felt so much gratitude before and she smiled at the grief of being torn between two worlds: this one and the next. As she continued to slip more into the unknown, simmering family dynamics and questions of morphine fell in and out of hearing. Her mind was going and the logical parameters or boundaries of what she thought was real were breaking apart. Talking and breathing were hard for her now and there was a strange, ironic humor in it all. Being ok with dying: thankful, gracious, and lingering with this life, but ready for what lay beyond the borders of the known, where she couldn't pick or choose. She realized that *this* life had always been this way.

In the midst of death, as all her opinions, thoughts, and beliefs melted away, a freedom beyond the scope of what she had previously experienced leaped towards her. She had lost her internal walls and so she stepped intimately into the life she had always been a part of:

> One day she awoke among dreams, pain, and memories, and asked aloud, "What day is it?"
>
> Her husband responded, "It's Tuesday dear, how are you feeling?"
>
> She had lost her sense of relationship with the outside world, or what she once thought of as reality. All that mattered to her now was that it was her time and that she was ready to move on. She said, "I'm supposed to be dead today dear!"

Later on she awoke again to see her granddaughter smiling holding her once- strong hands, hands that recalled setting sail across coral reef passages in the Seychelles and plucking rocket lettuce, tomatoes, and fresh chicken eggs from her bountiful Welsh garden, hands that had borne her children and grandchildren, hands that clasped her glass of white wine and slapped her thigh after a good laugh, hands that had touched and expressed so much in this world and that held fast so many dear ones to her heart.

Her granddaughter interrupted her thoughts and lovingly told her, "I'm going for a walk Nain. I will be back in a little bit."[2]

The Welsh grandmother was very tired, but she had not lost her spirit and her wild humor.

She lovingly responded, "If you tell me that you are going to see me when you get back, I'm going to throw something at you!"

The grandmother held on, slipping in and out of consciousness deep into the night and the following day. She passed away, leaving her family to grieve as she went out the back door.[3] There wasn't anything she or anyone else could do but accept the moment and appreciate the existence of a wonderful, vibrant life.

"If you tell me that you are going to see me when you get back, I'm going to throw something at you!" – reverberating outwards, her own fierce kindness was her *Way*.

---

[2] "Nain" is the Welsh word for grandmother.

[3] As the cliffs erode into the sea and eventually make their way down into the earth's mantle, so too do those we love. Going back into infinity is an inevitable step. Taking a creative approach to dying – facing it head on – one sneaks through the back door (There is a certain kind of playfulness embedded within this line. I often envision children playing hide and seek, sneaking away and leaping out the back door. It takes the heaviness of tragedy out of a natural event.).

The grandmother's death was hard on her family, but easy on the sky under which she lived. When she let go, it all became so clear. There was a reverence and an ancient wisdom that flowed out of her handling of an apparent impasse: taking the moment in hand and passing right through, without doing, picking, or choosing. She appears now and again in the laughter of her descendants and the winds that blow their sails through the calmest of mornings and the darkest of nights.

I often hear Sengcan's line jumping out of redwood tree roots, or the texture of frozen ice cream – intimate, yet tantalizing to the senses. I also see it within the Welsh grandmother's actions, a letting go and a dropping away of smallness to enter into what is, even if that "what is," is death. Meditating on this story brings out a spaciousness in my life and a kind of reverence for the greater movements of the universe. And then this fades into ordinariness, for that is what not picking and choosing is, inhabiting the ordinary mind and watching the unfurling of life without labeling or compartmentalizing it. Grounded into the sky, no matter the storm, what is… *is*.

Sengcan may not be in the past, eluding the roving intellectual flashlights of present-day scholars and Zen enthusiasts. He could be here now, sitting quietly on the veranda or emanating from the Welsh grandmother's open mind. He also may be in your mind too, watching a sunset or chuckling at an inside joke. Putting down our little minds and gleaning the lessons within the Sengcans floating through time and space, even those making brief appearances into our lives, opens up the possibilities for the innate

Sengcan mind within to come forth. And that mind is something to be experienced intimately too. It might not be about externalities – life, death, chocolate or strawberry, cream or white colored wall paint – it could be all about *You*: how open are you to the total, unfettered experience of *this* life?

About the author

Don Dianda is the author of *See for your Self: Zen Mindfulness for the Next Generation*. Through meditation, daily mindfulness practice, and individual koan work, Dianda seeks to shed light on the inherently deep connection one can have with the experience of *this* life as well as the world one moves through. You can see more of Don's work at:

http://redwoodzen.blogspot.com/

Photo taken by Alexi Papalexopoulos

Endnotes

[1] "The Buddha said, 'The past no longer exists, and the future is not here.' There is only a single moment in which we can be alive... Being present in the here and now is our practice" Thich Nhat Hanh, *You Are Here*.

[2] Zen Master Bankei taught Buddha-nature or Buddha mind as inherent within each being. Buddha-nature is of "one substance" and is the same among contemporaries as past Buddhas without any difference. Like the one water of the vast ocean, Buddha-nature is the substance (the water) that binds us. Those who are caught in the mirage of the waves: birth and death, good and bad, right and wrong, pass through life not knowing their true nature (Peter Haskel, *Bankei Zen*, p. 77–78 New York: Grove: 1984).

[3] Taken from the Diamond Sutra, "Out of nowhere, the mind comes forth"

[4] Stone wall: one who remains separate and enclosed – surrounded by his or her fixed positions, beliefs, and conceptualizations.

[5] The Way: "Look, and it can't be seen. Listen, and it can't be heard... Above, it isn't bright. Below, it isn't dark... Approach it and there is no beginning; follow it and there is no end. You can't know it but you can be it" (Stephen Mitchell's translation of the *Tao Te Ching*).

[6] The book is open – a taste: see for your Self. Yes, my experience is here and in a sense, the book is written to address me, but it can also be turned around and placed onto you. The fundamental issue here for the reader does not concern 'me' or how a master functions, but instead, how you function and who you are. What is there in you below the surface? "see for your Self" is just a mirror.

[7] No expectations! This is living.

[8] Right on the tip of one's nose...

[9] The italicized *"Right,"* refers to Buddha's Eightfold Path: *(1) Right View (2) Right Intention (3) Right Speech (4) Right Action (5) Right Livelihood (6) Right Effort (7) Right Mindfulness (8) Right Concentration.*

[10] The Three Afflictions: ignorance (how much we don't know), attachment (to ideas, religion, relationships, power, thoughts), and aversion (stemming from one's resistance to change).

[11] To focus on sex – not meaningful, deep sex that stems from total presence and a close relationship, instead, I focused on sex I couldn't even remember in the morning!

[12] Always succumbing to the voice in my head. You are not the voice!

[13] We have so many masks. Take them off one by one and reach down into your true Self.

[14] A cultural trait perhaps?

[15] Find the definition of 'Self' on page 43.

[16] An intimacy that is grounded in the image of fullness: that we, in the midst of infinity, are held up by the universe without any effort or control – we are here – we managed to be born and we will manage to go back when the time comes. All things between are like this: coming into the foreground from a giving, incalculably vast background, without our meddling.

[17] Not without pain or doubt

[18] An unconscious life

[19] When we are so attached to our bubbles, impermanence is an amazing realization.

[20] One's path: A life-long journey through the now.

[21] And thus that difficult for the complex mind, the layered ego...

22 "Zen does not confuse spirituality with thinking about God while one is peeling potatoes. Zen spirituality is just to peel the potatoes." – Alan Watts

23 My inability to inhabit the present-moment.

24 Gerald D. Fischbach, Scientific American, 1992

25 This description is in itself a conceptualization. At some point, we put it all down and walk into open space.

26 To the mind, the correct word might be "mystical" as opposed to "substantial."

27 The imagery of an iceberg can be applied here.

28 And they will come roaring back! This dynamic between the foreground and the background of our lives is our practice!

29 Pure awareness

30 small

31 Big

32 And then of course, we discover that nothing is far beyond our capacity because it is always right here on the edge of our noses.

33 The *Self*, which can be described as "Absolute," divine, or true Self, is who an individual is below the ego and the world it perceives. It is the Big Mind. The term "no-self" is thus a denial of the superficial ego-self as a means of connecting with the Absolute Self. The Absolute Self is synonymous with Buddha-nature. One can get a much deeper understanding of the Self through an example given in D.T. Suzuki's work: "The master said: 'The Buddha-nature (or Absolute Self) in its purity remains serene from the first and shows no movement whatever. It is free of all categories such as being and non-being, long and short, grasping and giving up, purity and defilement. It stands by itself in tranquility." (*The Awakening of Zen*, 94).

Rather than a being, the Self can be viewed as clear awareness. Remember, these are just definitions. When one directly experiences the vastness, nothing remains but the Now.

[34] It cannot be stressed enough that in the end the Self is yet another conceptualization made with the aim of describing something that cannot be described. You can look, you can see and directly experience what it is for your Self.

[35] The term "No-Self" can also be used to define the Self, in that it resembles infinite space in the here an now and thus is indefinable! Self, No-Self, Self, No-Self and so forth, it is ok to attach to one of these terms in the short term, but through practice and experience, Self and No-Self will become synonymous, and then, they will disappear into space.

[36] Turn the light back on itself

[37] St. John the Cross

[38] They don't call an attachment, 'an attachment,' for nothing.

[39] "Small doubt, small enlightenment, Big doubt, big enlightenment" – Korean Zen Master, Nine Mountains

[40] "In the pursuit of knowledge / every day something is added / In the practice of the Tao / every day something is dropped" (Tao Te Ching)

[41] Emptiness

[42] The ultimate form of transformation.

[43] From *The Transmission of the Lamp*

[44] If we really want to bring meditation to modern times, then think of meditation as an investment of time in yourself, an investment that will bring high dividends!

[45] *Zen Flesh, Zen Bones*

[46] I would refer to 'going beyond knowing' as stepping into ultimate reality.

47 I often carried Bodhidharma's line, "I don't know," with me ; "I felt free" could also be described as, "I felt weightless."

48 When emperor Wu asked Bodhidharma who he was, Bodhidharma replied, "I don't know." This exchange is one of the most cited koans.

49 Any attempt to label or corner what the experience of going beyond knowing is like, is false. We must be the ones to experience it for our Selves.

50 A natural process: something that can be very uncomfortable for some people!

51 Dropping his distinctions, his ego, his problems, his glory...

52 On his deathbed, a Zen master was asked by his disciples for a final phrase to sum up his life's teachings. He responded, "Attention, attention, attention!" D.T. Suzuki elaborates on the quote when he writes, "The only thing that is needed is to keep the eye wide open so that unnecessary ingredients do not obscure the reality itself... when one's inner urge is so strong and imperative there is no time or room left for deliberation" (*What is Zen*).

53 Using the Dharma

54 The breeze can come in and blow right through.

55 The logical – trying to understand – clouds it.

56 Nan-ch'üan asks Tao-wu, "What can you say about that place that knowledge does not reach?" Tao-wu replied, "One should absolutely avoid talking about that." Nan-ch'üan said, "Truly, as soon as one explains, horns sprout on one's head, and one becomes a beast."

57 Space is the key, but we must be open to receive what comes.

58 The front door opens and we are there to greet Andromeda, our neighboring Galaxy.

[59] Faith in one's Self and deepening into ultimate reality go hand-in-hand.

[60] Mirroring life.

[61] Paraphrase: "Without affirming or negating, What is it!?"

[62] Trusting in the infinite background and remaining tuned into this very moment breeds unobstructed, unforced, spontaneity.

[63] Metaphorically, one can view surrender as a way of removing the obstacles or objects in a stream that block the inherent flow downstream.

[64] Some would say, letting go of our stories, the little, subjective narratives that run our lives. Whether we have been wronged, harmed, or carried on top of a silver platter, our stories create a barrier between the infinite nature of the world/universe we move through, and us.

[65] The boogie man was not the boogie man, or if it was, it was as real as the hopes and fears deep within my mind.

[66] We are one. Greeting him and melting into one another, in this moment, is my practice.

[67] Though it may seem farfetched, there is a Buddha wrapped within the fog of every human being. Through practice and letting go, this reality cannot be denied – just suppressed.

[68] "If you turn things around, you are like the Buddha." Down and out can really mean a wonderful opportunity for inner growth and deep understanding.

[69] Delusion creates calm or chaos / enlightenment entails no good or evil... / If you don't fall asleep / dreams cease on their own accord." – Seng-ts'an (d. 606) *Relying on Mind*

[70] Note: Sitting hand-in-hand with the universe.

71 The Buddha said, "this saha world," which translates as the world of shifting forms that must be endured or experienced.

72 Buddha compared *this* life to a lightning bolt: one blink and the brilliant flash is gone.

73 In other words, we do not take in the whole picture – one that is so vast, it is impossible to grasp. It is our task to put down our small view of life and to be ok with what springs out of the vastness.

74 A reference to Socrates in Plato's Allegory of the Cave (*The Republic*)

75 "Like gravity, karma is so basic we often don't even notice it." - Sakyong Mipham

76 It takes years of practice to break through our own lives to become a Master. As I write these words, I imagine one of the ancients slashing though my words with a simple, "It is all shit, and all fan!" – crushing all conceptualizations and explanations with one stroke! The beauty of Zen practice is just that, to go beyond karma through slicing off thought and reaction – melting into the background.

77 Though we often think of ourselves as intelligent beings that are separate from the earth and the animals that roam upon it – this is pure delusion. We come from nature. We go to nature to pay our respect, to be rejuvenated and to feel a greater appreciation for the mystery that goes beyond all concepts, judgments, and rationalizations. Nature is the pure manifestation of the Tao and we can better understand the Tao by sitting and watching nature unfold moment after moment.

78 A more accurate word than "learn" would be "unlearn."

79 The earth is our mother: fundamentally the place where we are all born.

80 Placed perfectly away from the sun – not too hot, not too cold – shielded by the great asteroid belt, the earth is a gem and we are very fortunate to be its inhabitants.

81 We can focus in on death – carnivores and herbivores, volcanoes and disease – but to see the small without seeing the large, we lose the truth. Each piece has its role to play in maintaining the overall *One*.

82 Zen Master Dogen

83 This sentence is a fundamental part of letting go: The unpredictable, wide-open nature of life can be realized in a single stroke! Or, through thousands of small strokes over many years – wind removing grain after grain of sand from the castles we have built our entire lives.

84 The discomfort of not knowing or being able to control is unacceptable to the logical mind lost in the haze of labeling.

85 If a Master blows out our little candle and leaves us in the dark, will we understand, will we be open?

86 A monk asked, "What is the treasure in the bag?" The Master replied, "Keep your mouth closed." Keep it simple.

87 I think it is very important to note that we may trick ourselves into believing that we are farther along the path than we actually are in this moment. This is a forward leaning book that focuses on the gifts of practicing Zen mindfulness. While moving between the darkness and light, take inventory and do not sell yourself short. There may be past grievances that had a powerful effect on your life and that need more time and conscious awareness. I am still in this arena and I invite you to join me if you are walking through wild territory.

88 The mental map is a metaphor for our small mind: projecting, planning and creating our subjective reality.

When we let go of our small selves, relinquishing or surrendering the map, we enter into the stream – the flow.

[89] Again, koan: Student, "Where is the treasure in the bag?" Master: "Close your mouth."

[90] "To say that 'the Buddha appears in the world and saves sentient beings' are words of the nine-part teachings; they are words of the incomplete teaching. Anger and joy, sickness and medicine, are all oneself; there is no one else. Where is there a Buddha appearing in the world? Where are the sentient beings to be saved? As the *Diamond-Cutter Scripture* says, 'In reality, there are no sentient beings who attain extinction and deliverance.' " – Zen Master Pai-chang

[91] Something Buddha never wished for

[92] Stay involved, learn, morph, experience the now through and through and thus embody your Self through and through. That is the goal – that is what turning in is all about.

[93] Even this is going too far!

[94] "Bodhisattvas who practice transcendent wisdom should not grasp my words or depend on the commands of the teachings"

[95] How about now? Or... Now?

[96] "When there is no abiding of thought anywhere on anything - this is being unbound. This not abiding anywhere, is the root of our life" – Master Hui-neng

~

Made in the USA
San Bernardino, CA
15 December 2013